# The *Christian Life* Collection

# The Christian Life Collection

By Reinhard Bonnke

with George Canty

The Christian Life Collection
English
Copyright © CfaN 2005
ISBN 9764906-1-7

Edition 1, Printing 1
4,000 copies

Published by Christ for all Nations
P.O. Box 590588, Orlando, FL, 32859-0588
United States

Dust Jacket Photograph © Getty images

Previously published as separate booklets:

Assurance of Salvation
ISBN 3-935057-11-3

The Power of the Blood of Jesus
ISBN 3-935057-10-5

The Holy Spirit Baptism
ISBN 3-935057-12-1

The Lord your Healer
ISBN 3-935057-14-8

How to Receive a Miracle from God
ISBN 3-935057-13-X

First of all Intercession
ISBN 3-935057-17-2

Faith for the Night
ISBN 3-935057-16-4

The Romance of Redeeming Love
ISBN 3-935057-15-6

Winning your Friends & Family to Christ
ISBN 0-9758789-3-X

Visit the CfaN website at www.CfaN.org

Printed in China
www.china-print.com.cn

# CONTENTS

# ASSURANCE *of* SALVATION

# ASSURANCE OF SALVATION

## PERFECTLY CERTAIN

When you are saved, you should know it. Otherwise, how can you be a witness for Christ? The Bible speaks clearly and positively; it does not stammer. When you read it, you become certain. Martin Luther once said, "The Holy Spirit is no skeptic." He writes no doubts. The promises of God are *Yes and Amen* (2 Corinthians 1:20) and not No or Maybe. The Gospel trumpet sounds no faltering note.

When an earthquake shook the Philippian jail and all who were in it, the jailor cried out, *What must I do to be saved?* Paul did not say, "Well, what do you think? Do you have any ideas?" He made a firm statement of fact in Acts 16:31: *Believe on the Lord Jesus Christ, and you will be saved.* The Gospel is God's message, not Christian opinion.

> *When you repent and believe and come to the Lord and Savior Jesus Christ, He receives you, and you are cleansed in His precious blood!*

The genius who made the first electric dynamo, Michael Faraday, was not only a master of all the sciences, but also a Christian. In 1867, when he was dying, his friends asked him what his speculations about life after death were. "Speculations?" he asked in surprise. "Speculations! I have none. I am resting on certainties!" Faraday's favorite Bible verse was: *I know whom I have believed, and am persuaded that he is able to keep that which I have committed unto him against that day* (2 Timothy 1:12 AV). He had no reservations about biblical truth.

Some people argue that it is presumptuous to declare you are saved, but that is false modesty in the light of so much scriptural evidence. When Christ confronts you with the question of your need, you should not respond, "I want to have my questions answered and to give my view of salvation." Instead, you must repent and believe! Being saved is not a casual experience, something you would hardly notice. When you repent and believe and come to the Lord and Savior Jesus Christ, He receives you, and you are cleansed in His precious blood! Take these two statements made by Christ Jesus: *All that the Father gives Me will come to Me, and the one who comes to Me I will by no means cast out* (John 6:37) and *for the Son of Man has come to seek and to save that which was lost* (Luke 19:10).

Salvation is absolute and complete. How ridiculous to think that Jesus would find you and receive you, but would not want you to know this! In fact, He would not keep it from you. Another Scripture proves that: *The Spirit Himself bears witness with our spirit that we are children of God* (Romans 8:16).

## SATAN'S LACK OF EVIDENCE

Let me tell you, there is something greater still: You are *justified freely by His grace* (Romans 3:24). What a fantastic statement!

Such a thing could never happen to a lawbreaker in a court of law. Imagine it: The courtroom with serious looking officials, the uniformed police, the prosecutor, and judge. The jury returns with a verdict of guilty. The defendant stands in the dock condemned. He must suffer the penalty, and pay the price. If he asked to be justified, the solemn court would burst into disbelieving laughter.

Now picture a different scene: A sinner stands before the highest Judge of all. The accuser, Satan, is there, and dazzling ranks of sinless angels look on. The sinner knows he is guilty. The Judge of all the earth must act justly. The sinner's Advocate, Jesus, appears and challenges the accuser, "Where is your evidence?"

That causes quite a stir! The accuser is embarrassed. He cannot produce any evidence, no damning exhibit, no deposition, and no record. Not a single scrap of proof. No sign of this man's wrongdoing can be discovered in the entire universe. What has happened to it?

I will tell you: Our sinful evidence has been destroyed! Christ Jesus gathered it all unto Himself and carried it into the fires of divine judgment, which swept across Calvary. During those awful hours, the record was consumed, leaving no trace. Colossians 2:13-14 describes it:

> And you, being dead in your trespasses and the uncircumcision of your flesh, He has made alive together with Him, having forgiven you all trespasses, having wiped out the handwriting of requirements that was against us, which was contrary to us. And He has taken it out of the way, having nailed it to the cross.

In the court of God, Jesus the Advocate makes His sensational claim, "There is no evidence against this man." Then the throne of justice becomes the throne of grace. Satan the accuser retires in baffled rage. The Judge beckons the accused and hands him a document called 'The New Covenant.' He opens it. There he sees that it carries the red seals of the sprinkled blood of Jesus. It is a royal exoneration declaring, "This court finds no evidence and therefore no case against you." *There is therefore now no condemnation to those who are in Christ Jesus, who do not walk according to the flesh, but according to the Spirit* (Romans 8:1). The Judge has signed it saying, *"Their sins and their lawless deeds I will remember no more"* (Hebrews 10:17).

The prisoner is free, justified by grace. Then the whole court rises and applauds, for there is joy in heaven over one sinner that repents (Luke 15:7). When you are justified by grace, God the Judge wants you to know it. Those who wait for the Day of Judgment to discover whether they are saved or damned do not understand salvation at all. Knowing the promise of Jesus in John 5:24, that you *shall not come into judgment* is part of salvation. He lifts that fear from you when you get saved.

> **When you are justified by grace, God the Judge wants you to know it.**

The word judgment in that Scripture is the Greek word '*krisis*,' from which the word crisis is derived. So you can say that a born-again believer will never know such a 'crisis' hour, standing in the judgment, waiting to find out whether he is saved or lost. The matter is already settled.

## THE GAUGE

What a strange thing, then, that even some church members seem unsure about their fate and do not expect to learn until the great Day of Judgment! They use the words perhaps and hope. God says, *"He who believes in the Son of God has the witness in himself ... these things I have written to you who believe in the name of the Son of God, that you may know that you have eternal life"* (1 John 5:10, 13).

Note that these reassuring Scriptures do not say that you WILL have eternal life, but they say you already HAVE it – now! These are powerful promises, which the apostle John received from the Holy Spirit. They contain the key elements about the assurance of salvation: written; believe; Son of God; know; have; eternal life. These keys are given in the Word of God, which means you must read what is written in the Word.

The biblical principle is that every matter must be established by the testimony of two or three witnesses. Assurance is so important that God has given it a double anchorage in the rock of two faultless witnesses, both divine: THE WORD OF GOD AND THE SPIRIT OF GOD.

# WITNESS NUMBER ONE

## THE WORD OF GOD

Many people want assurance to register in their feelings. This is a common mistake, which often has a disastrous outcome. God never said that your emotions would be the test of your salvation. Assurance is not dependent on your psyche, but on His eternal Word. Although the human soul is a masterpiece of creation, it was made to fluctuate with experience, registering ups and downs, being glad, or being sad, according to your state of mind, EVEN AFTER YOU ARE SAVED. Saved people do not have ever-smiling faces, like plastic masks, but they have entered God's original plan for their lives and have no need to consult their emotions to determine whether they are saved or not.

*Salvation is embedded in the rock of the eternal Word of God.*

So, salvation is embedded in the rock of the eternal Word. Jesus stated: *Heaven and earth will pass away, but My words will by no means pass away* (Matthew 24:35). This is the cleft in the rock to which you must flee whenever Satan attacks you with doubts. You are saved because the Word of God says you are. Whatever I feel, my conviction remains unshakable.

The first Christians were not uncertain. Scripture says that they were abounding *in hope by the power of the Holy Spirit* (Romans 15:13), having an *abundance of joy* (2 Corinthians 8:2), and an *abundance of grace* (Romans 5:17). Abounding means enough and some to spare, a surplus, like the twelve baskets of food left over after Jesus fed the five thousand (Matthew 14:1-21).

> *Assurance of salvation is not over-confidence, but a deep, settled peace, which fills your soul in moments when the devil whispers doubts.*

Assurance of salvation is not over-confidence, but a deep, settled peace, which fills your soul in moments when the devil whispers doubts.

Paul described Christians in Colosse as having *all riches of the full assurance* (Colossians 2:2). Riches of assurance! That word riches in the original Greek is '*ploutos*,' the root of the word '*plutocrat*,' which means somebody who reigns by his wealth. I do not mind being a spiritual *plutocrat*, being WEALTHY IN CONFIDENCE IN GOD. The letter to the Hebrews speaks of *full assurance* (Hebrews 6:11, 10:22), and in Thessalonica they had *much assurance* (1 Thessalonians 1:5), literally 'much fullness.' That is the true fullness, being rich in faith towards God.

## RINGING CONFIDENCE

The whole New Testament rings with confidence. Peter spoke positively when preaching in Jerusalem, *Let all the house of Israel know assuredly that God has made this Jesus, whom you crucified, both Lord and Christ* (Acts 2:36). He later brought the news about the conversion of the Gentiles and said that *God, who knows the heart, acknowledged them by giving them the Holy Spirit* (Acts 15:8).

The Ephesians received the 'guarantee' of their spiritual inheritance and were 'sealed' with the Holy Spirit (Ephesians 1:13-14, 4:30). What a contrast to nervous indecision! The Corinthians were told: *We have received ... the Spirit who is from God, that we might know the things that have been freely given to us by God* (1 Corinthians 2:12).

Any doctrine, which leaves you guessing about your soul's salvation, is completely out of harmony with the New Testament. Paul told the skeptics of Athens that God *has given assurance of this to all by raising Him* (Jesus) *from the dead* (Acts 17:31).

You do not have to guard your salvation as if it would disappear if you were careless. You do not have to save your salvation. The Lord preserves your soul!

If you want even more proof, read the epistles of John. In one short letter he uses two Greek verbs normally translated '*know*' forty-two times, like this: *Now by this we know that we know Him ... by this we know that we are in Him ... you know all things ... we know that we have passed from death to life ... we know love ... we know that we are of the truth ... you know the Spirit of God ... we know that we abide in Him* and so on (1 John 2:3-5.20).

> *You do not have to guard your salvation as if it would disappear if you were careless.*

This does not make Christians know-it-alls. Salvation does not depend on intelligence or analysis of abstract theological concepts. In fact, Jesus rejoices because He can say to His Father in heaven, *You have hidden these things from the wise and prudent and have revealed them to babes* (Matthew 11:25).

To be sure of salvation, you do not need to be sure of everything, but only of God, who *is faithful and just to forgive us our sins, and to cleanse us from all unrighteousness* (1 John 1:9). *He who promised is faithful* (Hebrews 10:23).

Let me use a simple illustration. I am Reinhard Bonnke, whether I feel like it or not. If I am asleep, I do not think about it, but I am still Reinhard Bonnke. Even if I should suffer from a loss of memory, my identity remains the same – I am still Reinhard Bonnke. My birth certificate states that I am who I am, and that settles it.

> *The Bible is your birth certificate. If you cannot believe that, then you will not know who you are.*

So it is with the Word of God. If you have received the Lord Jesus Christ as your personal Savior, you have been born into the family of God ... BORN AGAIN. The Bible is your birth certificate. If you cannot believe that, then you will not know who you are ... it is that simple! John said: *Beloved, now we are children of God; and it has not yet been revealed what we shall be* (1 John 3:2).

What we shall be we do not yet perceive, but we know who we are – we are children of God. Jesus said:

> *Most assuredly, I say to you, he who hears My word and believes in Him who sent Me has everlasting life, and shall not come into judgment, but has passed from death into life.* (John 5:24)

That is powerful! It says that if you HAVE repented and HAVE received Jesus as your own Savior, then you HAVE everlasting life and HAVE crossed over from death to life. Praise the Lord!

## THE WORD OF THE CROSS

When the apostle Paul preached in Corinth, he did not feel physically robust and full of vigor. He was weak and trembling (1 Corinthians 2:3). His preaching was simple and direct. He did not go storming in, relying on brilliant speech to overwhelm his hearers, yet he preached *in the demonstration of the Spirit and of power* (1 Corinthians 2:4). The effects were mighty and many repented and received salvation. How could that be? What did he preach to have such effects? The secret is this: He said: *For I determined not to know anything among you, except Jesus Christ, and Him crucified* (1 Corinthians 2:2).

The Gospel is the Word of God, Peter said, and that Gospel is the Word of the Cross. Salvation is not a theory. It does not rest in mere words, not even in stirred emotions, but on what happened, on a fact, a deed. *Christ died for our sins according to the Scriptures* (1 Corinthians 15:3).

If you want assurance that TODAY God smiles upon you and is on your side, and that one day you will be welcomed in heaven, this is how it happens:

1. First, you hear or read the Gospel that Christ died for your sins.

2. Next, you believe the Gospel and repent, and the power of God applies the benefits of Christ's redeeming death to your heart.

3. Then, something wonderful happens: The Word of God quickens your dead spirit, and you become alive in God, cleansed and made whole. What Jesus did for you on the cross, the Holy Spirit transfers into your life.

Let me illustrate this: You may have electricity in your home. The house is wired and connected to the power plant. If you go home on a dark night, there is no light or heat there, but you know what to do: you press the switch, and power comes through. You have instant light and warmth.

Believing that Christ died for you is like turning the switch on. Everything else is ready. The Gospel message is like the wires and cables that are connected to the power station – Calvary's Cross. The lines of truth have already been laid. The power is there waiting. Then you believe, which turns on the spiritual switch, and the saving power flows to you, giving you light. You are saved.

Some people seem to know all about the Cross. They wear a cross or carry a crucifix. But it is merely a superstition, which does nothing for them. Knowing all about a power station can still leave you in the cold and dark. You can touch the very walls of a nuclear power plant, but still be freezing. Yet you can plug in to the power of God because the preaching of the Gospel, the truth, completes the wiring system. When you hear it and believe it, you are tapping in to the resources of God, which are inexhaustible. Then you KNOW that you are saved.

## THE CONQUEROR WITH THE BLEEDING FEET

There were people actually at the foot of the Cross, while Jesus hung there, but they were not saved. The Bible describes some who *sitting down, they kept watch over Him there* (Matthew 27:36). That is all they did, so they were not saved.

Today, thousands of people do the same thing. They are just onlookers, curious perhaps, or even pitying, feeling sorry about Christ's death, but never receiving what He died to give them: an assurance of God's forgiveness and His acceptance of them.

When faith comes, assurance comes. You cannot separate them, and sometimes in Scripture the two words are exactly the same. I want to show you how this can be. We read in Mark 15:29, 32, that *those who passed by blasphemed Him, wagging their heads and saying ... let the Christ, the King of Israel, descend now from the cross, that we may see and believe.* They actually saw Jesus dying for them, but they did not believe and were not saved.

> **When faith comes, then assurance comes. You cannot separate them.**

See and believe! Mark had his answer to that. He writes that one man, a Roman centurion, was different. *So when the centurion, who stood opposite Him, saw that He cried out like this and breathed His last, he said, "Truly this Man was the Son of God!"* (Mark 15:39). This soldier had seen the whole thing, and with a more perceiving eye, saw the truth.

He did not need to see a wonder, a miracle, or a display of magic, like Christ detaching Himself from the nails and walking around, or Elijah coming to release Jesus, as some had hoped. He was seeing the true wonder, the love of God, and the greatness of Christ. He saw the glory of God in the face of Jesus Christ.

The crowds had more than once wanted Jesus to be king, and to conquer the much-hated Roman army of occupation. But He refused. His servants did not fight to make Him an earthly lord. He had a new way. Jesus conquered this Roman who was in charge of the squad of soldiers that carried out executions. Nailed and helpless, yet Christ conquered this military commander. Within three hundred years, Rome itself had been conquered, not by the jackbooted feet of military forces, but by the bleeding feet of this Man hanging there. O praise the Lord!

The last pagan emperor, named Julian, tried to restore the old worship of the gods, but the tides released by Christ's death were too powerful. Julian cried out in agony, "O Galilean, you have conquered!"

## THE ANCHOR AND THE FORERUNNER

To *see and believe* means to see Jesus tasting death for every man and for you. The Cross stands fast. It is an *anchor of the soul*. This figure of speech is found in Hebrews 6:19-20: *This hope we have as an anchor of the soul, both sure and steadfast, and which enters the Presence behind the veil, where the forerunner has entered for us, even Jesus.*

There is a seagoing picture from those ancient days: A ship comes into harbor, but cannot draw too near the shore in the darkness. So a sailor gets into a boat with an anchor and a line connecting ship and anchor. He is called the 'forerunner.' As he rows, the line linking anchor and ship is played out. Eventually, the forerunner's boat reaches the shore, and the seaman secures the anchor on land.

In the morning, the ship needs no sails. The crew of the ship begins to wind in the anchor cable. However, it is not the anchor that moves but the ship. Slowly the vessel is winched towards the shore. This is the origin of the word forerunner.

Your forerunner is Jesus, who has entered through the veil and made fast your anchor. Your salvation is secured like the anchor ashore, which the crew cannot see. Christ is no longer visible to you; He is 'ashore' in glory, and YOU ARE ATTACHED, BY FAITH, TO HIM. He has entered glory for you. Day by day the cable is shortening and pulling you nearer and nearer to Christ, your forerunner.

Eventually you will reach heaven's shore, and what will you see? Your forerunner waiting to greet you, to *receive you to Myself; that where I am, there you may be also* (John 14:3). Faith links you already and will bring you to Him at last. That faith is assurance.

> We have an anchor that keeps the soul
> Steadfast and sure while the billows roll.
> Fasten'd to the Rock which cannot move,
> Grounded firm and deep in the Savior's love!

## HOW TO ROUT DOUBT

I said that Paul's feelings in Corinth were of weakness and trembling. He even feared for his mortal life. Nevertheless he knew! God was with him. He was often *struck down*, as he said in 2 Corinthians 4:9, and *despaired even of life* (2 Corinthians 1:8), but it left his assurance of hope absolutely unaffected.

Do you know that the devil can bring on lying feelings? If he does not succeed in confusing you with lying words, he resorts to depressing your emotions. However, remember the Bible's warning that Satan is the father of lies (John 8:44); he is a master at the game. Some people feel saved one day and not the next, but the day after that it seems as if their salvation has come back. All feelings. If you do not believe Satan's lying words, do not believe the lying feelings he gives you either.

What should you do? The answer is:

1. Go to the Word of God.

2. Find a Scripture like John 5:24.

3. Read it over and over again.

*Most assuredly, I say to you, he who hears My word and believes in Him who sent Me has everlasting life, and shall not come into judgment, but has passed from death into life.* (John 5:24)

The Word is your birth certificate. God says you are His child, you have eternal life, and that Word is never wrong. You will not be lost. You just believe it, and believe it you must!

A little boy had received Jesus as his Savior at Sunday School. His teacher had hammered John 5:24 into him, and he had underlined it in his New Testament. That night he got into bed, read his Bible, prayed and switched off the light. Then the devil came bringing doubts, suggesting that he was not saved. The boy quickly switched on the light and read John 5:24 again. He was happy that the Bible had not changed! It still said he HAD eternal life. Once more, he switched off the light, and again doubt came back. This time, he said, it was as if it came from under his bed. Once more, he switched on the light, and turning again to John 5:24, held his New Testament under the bed and said, "Look, devil, if you don't believe me, then read it for yourself: I HAVE PASSED FROM DEATH TO LIFE. I AM A CHILD OF GOD!"

The Word of God silences the accuser and routs our doubts. As the hymn says:

> How firm a foundation, ye saints of the Lord,
> Is laid for your faith in His excellent Word!
> What more can He say than to you He hath said,
> You who unto Jesus for refuge have fled?

The Word is the sure anchor that God has given you for the times of storm, and will secure you in life and in death.

So then, believe what God has said in His holy Word because, *without faith it is impossible to please Him, for he who comes to God must believe that He is, and that He is a rewarder of those who diligently seek Him* (Hebrews 11:6).

# WITNESS NUMBER TWO

## THE SPIRIT OF GOD

After you have believed what the Word of God says about the certainty of your salvation through Jesus Christ, and only after, the Holy Spirit becomes active in your life: *The Spirit Himself bears witness with our spirit that we are children of God* (Romans 8:16).

Note that the Bible uses the word spirit twice, once with a capital letter denoting God's Spirit, and once with a small letter denoting the human spirit. God's Spirit witnesses to your human spirit that you ARE A CHILD OF GOD. You are a partaker of the divine nature (2 Peter 1:4), and your new heart tells you that God is your Father. Then, suddenly, you have a close relationship with Him and cry, *Abba, Father* (Galatians 4:6). This settles the matter completely, because then even your feelings will adjust to the testimony of the Holy Spirit within you.

In any case, the key is, that after repentance and faith, you BELIEVE the Word of God; otherwise, you can never even start being sure of your salvation. It says there that God calls you His child, so you can be certain He is your Father, and all other believers are your brothers and sisters. This puts the whole family of God together, without distinction or discrimination by race, or wisdom, or age, or education, on earth or in heaven. Glory be to God!

If people try to show off their learning by posing weighty problems, in order to display their 'intellectual honesty,' Jesus simply says that they *are mistaken, not knowing the Scriptures nor the power of God* (Matthew 22:29). Logic cannot possibly embrace the dimension of eternal salvation, which comes from the mind and heart of God. You cannot put God in a test tube.

## THE SECRETARY OF THE TRINITY

I once heard someone say that the Holy Spirit is the 'Secretary of the Trinity.' When I thought about it, I had to agree. A secretary's work is to communicate the decisions of the board to the people concerned. And now, after you have received Jesus as your Savior, the Holy Spirit immediately swings into action. A registered letter arrives, as it were, at the door of your heart with a fantastic message.

This illustration sums up the truth of Romans 8:16. It is exactly what it means. How wonderful!

Dear Reader, If you have received Jesus Christ as your personal Savior, then write your name on the dotted line on the next page, because this letter is personally addressed to you!

*Dear ............................................................,*

*I have been advised by the Father and the Son to inform you that your sins are forgiven and blotted out[1].*

*Furthermore, I have been instructed to let you know that your name has been written in the Lamb's Book of Life in heaven[2].*

*I am to exhort you to be faithful unto death[3], because an incorruptible crown and inheritance are waiting for you in heaven[4].*

*Finally, I am to urge you to be strong in the Lord and in the power of His might[5]!*

*Yours most faithfully and ever-abidingly[6],*

*On behalf of the Trinity,*

*THE HOLY SPIRIT*

---

[1] Colossians 2:14    [2] Luke 10:20
[3] Revelation 2:10    [4] 1 Peter 1:3-5
[5] Ephesians 6:10     [6] John 14:16

## THE HOLY SPIRIT'S GREATEST WORK

Salvation is the Holy Spirit's greatest work. It does not bring about only minor results, like patching you up, making you religious, or tuning you in to nature.

The creation of heaven and earth took God just six days to complete, but He spent centuries preparing for mankind's salvation.

> *The creation of heaven and earth took God just six days to complete, but He spent centuries preparing for mankind's salvation.*

He was working in different locations ... Egypt, Israel, Babylon, and Rome ... through good men and bad, throughout history until, Jesus came in *the fullness of the time*, (Galatians 4:4). It affected everything and everyone, even God. God's Son, torn from His side, depriving angels of their joy, faced life from the humble stable in Bethlehem. Then He faced death on Calvary, making war on Satan. In that struggle the earth was shaken, the rocks rent, the sun blacked out of the sky. Cowed by such awesome scenes, His enemies, who had howled like wolves for His blood, crept away in fear.

Hell felt the impact. Jesus Christ broke out of the granite of the sealed tomb, unhinging the gates of death, leading out captives and ascending far above all authorities to present His wounds to the Father. Wounded for me!

These are the mighty events, which made your and my salvation possible. It is too big a thing for you not to know you are saved! It is not just being hopeful or optimistic. The Word of God says it. Paul said: *I know whom I have believed and am persuaded* (2 Timothy 1:12).

# NO IMITATIONS

One additional point is important. *Nevertheless the solid foundation of God stands, having this seal: "The Lord knows those who are His," and, "Let everyone who names the name of Christ depart from iniquity"* (2 Timothy 2:19).

There is a false confidence, a false security that shows in arrogance, boasting of an experience of salvation, which never shows in a person's character, behavior, and life style. *You will know them by their fruits* (Matthew 7:16). Such people are phony Christians. *We know that we have passed from death to life, because we love the brethren. He who does not love his brother abides in death* (1 John 3:14).

There is a subtle danger. People can be imitators and live like Christians, but not be saved. Some people have pet parrots. Parrots are born mimics. A friend of mine has a fine African gray, named Polly, which repeats what people say, seemingly in their own voices. Sometimes it is hard to tell who is speaking. The bird talks as if it was one of the family, and uses a human-sounding voice. It tries to join in the conversation quite often. But alas, poor Polly ... though it talks like a human being and maybe even thinks it is one, it is still only a parrot.

Plenty of people live like Christians by imitation. They do what Christians are supposed to do. They parrot all the words but not the music, none of that glorious song of the redeemed responding to heaven. Their lives are all works and effort. They might be pretty good mimics, too, doing better than real Christians sometimes. But are they Christians? Christians are *partakers of the divine nature* (2 Peter 1:4), being born-again from above, their true spiritual Father being in heaven. They sing, "The Spirit answers to the blood and tells me I am born of God." When you are truly His, you should know it.

Now you may fail, but salvation goes on working in you to overcome your weaknesses. Your desire to please the Lord must be true, at least until the day when your redemption is completed, and you see His wonderful face. Until then, whatever comes, you can say as Paul said: *I am persuaded that He is able to keep what I have committed to Him until that Day* (2 Timothy 1:12).

დ

# THE POWER *of the* BLOOD *of* JESUS

# PREFACE

Having repeatedly seen a divine vision of a blood-washed Africa, I now desire nothing more than to see its glorious fulfillment. I vowed to God that I would preach the message of the Blood of Jesus Christ wherever He sends us. By the grace of God, we have made good progress over the years and seen many nations in Africa shaken by the power of the Gospel. Millions of precious souls have received Jesus Christ as their personal Savior. Sometimes I feel rather like a New Testament priest who carries the blood of Jesus in a bowl from nation to nation.

This message is powerful: it sets people free from sin, bondage, and fear.

# THE POWER OF
# THE BLOOD OF JESUS

There is power and redemption for everyone in the blood of Jesus Christ. A Buddhist told me that she could not understand how that could be. "Maybe," she said, "one man could die for a hundred, or at most for a thousand people, but never for all mankind."

Not only Buddhists, but also people of many religions find the teaching of forgiveness through the blood of Jesus revolutionary. People generally expect to pay for their sins, either now or in some other existence. The Christian revelation is the glorious fact that JESUS HAS PAID IT ALL. Our doubts are traitors when they prevent us from proving the power of Christ's cleansing blood.

> "Therefore let it be known to you, brethren, that through this Man [Jesus] is preached to you the forgiveness of sins," announced the apostle Paul. (Acts 13:38)

True forgiveness is as substantial as the cross on which Christ bought it. No man can understand forgiveness unless taught by experience. If the joy of it could be communicated, some would consider it too wonderful to be true. They can be assured, however, that divine forgiveness is not a fairy tale, or the fulfillment of some wish. It rests on a rock-solid foundation, on the historic fact of Jesus Christ's redemptive sacrifice. He suffers, *the just for the unjust, that He might bring us to God* (1 Peter 3:18). The Cross was no fiction. Real blood fell on real ground. And this real blood brings real cleansing to real sinners, and does much more besides.

I want to explain some of the very special facts about the blood of Jesus, and what benefits come to us by means of it. The deeper we look into the Word of God, the more awesome and glorious this truth becomes.

## APPLY THE BLOOD

In the entire Bible, no blood except the blood of Jesus is called *precious* (1 Peter 1:19). Millions of animals have been slaughtered to atone for sin, but their blood was not precious. The Old Testament sacrifices of Israel were simply poured away at the sides of the altars – powerless.

Suppose you have a table with a big stain on its surface. When visitors come, you cover the stain with a tablecloth, so that nobody will notice it. The stain is covered, but not removed. This is the meaning of the Old Testament word 'atonement' – covered. The rivers of blood of the millions of sacrificial animals were not able to 'take away' sin, but only to cover it for a while. That is the reason why John the Baptist was so excited when he saw Jesus come to the river Jordan, and cried,

> *Behold! The Lamb of God who takes away the sin of the world!* (John 1:29)

Jesus' blood works under the 'tablecloth' and behind every facade. It tackles the root sins and problems of all people who put their faith in Jesus Christ. The blood of the Lamb of God alone has value and power to save. His sacrifice was sufficient for all men, women, boys, and girls, no matter how old they are.

When Jesus walked on earth and delivered people from the oppression of Satan, that old deceiver watched Him. The blind saw and cripples walked. Christ destroyed the works of the devil systematically. Satan ground his teeth with rage and plotted to destroy the Lord Jesus Christ. He inspired evil men to crucify Christ. He gloated as they nailed down those wonderful hands of mercy. Those hands would give him no more trouble, he thought. It was all over. What a mistake Satan made! The very blood that he caused to be spilled now breaks the stranglehold of Satan upon men and women everywhere!

An atheist once challenged me on a television program. He said, "I do not believe that there is any power in the blood of Jesus. The blood of Jesus has been around for 2,000 years, and if there was any power in it, as you claim, the world would not be in such a sorry state."

I replied, "Sir, there is also plenty of soap around, yet many people are still dirty. Soap doesn't make anybody clean by just being around, not even if he works in a soap factory. If you want to know what soap can do you have TO TAKE IT AND APPLY IT PERSONALLY. Then you will see! That is how it is with the blood of Jesus. It is not enough to know about the blood, sing about it, or preach about it. I now challenge you, sir," I said. "Apply the blood of Jesus to your sinful life, and you will join hundreds of millions of people all over the world who sing and say,

There is power, power,
Wonder-working power
In the Blood of the Lamb."

## BLOOD DIFFERENT FROM ALL OTHER BLOOD

Our blood is ordinary, but the blood of Jesus is holy blood. There is power in the blood of Jesus because no man who ever lived had blood like His. The blood of Jesus is holy simply because the Bible calls it 'precious,' but there are also some other very interesting factors.

Everybody inherits blood group factors at conception. Jesus did not. Normally a blood test can prove whether or not a particular man was the father of a child. The blood of a child and of his true father can be checked scientifically for some genetic connection[1].

*Our blood is ordinary, but the blood of Jesus is holy blood.*

However, with Jesus there is a new situation: He had no earthly father! His blood could not be grouped because it was singular. It was independent of any genetic inheritance. The father of Jesus was the Father in heaven. The Bible is very careful to explain this. God inspired Luke, *the beloved physician* (Colossians 4:14), to tell us the facts, which he probably learned from Mary, the mother of Christ. She could speak without embarrassment to a doctor, so Luke gives us this report:

> *Then Mary said to the angel, "How can this be, since I do not know a man?" And the angel answered her and said to her, "The Holy Spirit will come upon you, and the power of the Highest will overshadow you; therefore, also, that Holy One who is to be born will be called the Son of God"* (Luke 1:34-35)

---

[1] Fifteen types of human blood groups have been noted, including a number of groupings that occur only in rare families. Dr. James V. Linman says, "A single system may involve one or several antigens or blood group factors. An infinite number of combinations is possible, and it seems likely that a person's precise blood type is as individually specific as are his fingerprints." (Dr. James V. Linman, *Hematology*, p. 976) Studies of what is known as the Rhesus factor have also shown that a mother can have Rh positive blood and her baby Rh negative. The mother's blood supports the unborn child through the placenta, which also prevents her blood entering the veins of her baby, unless damage causes a leak (Drs. S. Bender and V. R. Tindall, *Practical Student Obstetrics*, p. 40; Dr. Ian Donald, *Practical Obstetric Problems*, p. 981).

Mary and Joseph were engaged but had not yet come together as husband and wife. A virgin, Mary conceived by a miracle of God. Therefore Christ did not have blood group factors from Joseph or Joseph's ancestors. Jesus Christ is *the only begotten of the Father* (John 1:14).

With regard to Mary's blood type, we know that a woman can bear a child, which has a blood group completely incompatible with her own. In the womb, a child develops its own blood, which may be the opposite type to that of its mother. THE BLOOD OF JESUS WAS HIS OWN DIVINE BLOOD, AND THIS IS THE SECRET OF ITS POWER!

Only one other man ever had blood that was not genetically received: Adam, the first man, mentioned in Luke 3:38 as *of God*, that is, a special creation without any ancestor. The Bible calls Jesus *the last Adam* (1 Corinthians 15:45). His body, like the first Adam's, was specially *prepared*, as the Bible says (Hebrews 10:5). God caused Mary to bear a son without the normal biological necessities, for nothing is impossible for God[2].

However, there is a vast difference between the first Adam and the second Adam:

> *The first man was of the earth, made of dust; the second man is the Lord from heaven.* (1 Corinthians 15:47)

Adam's sin-contamination runs in the veins of us all, but for the above-mentioned reasons, it did not run in the veins of Jesus. His blood is holy.

---

[2] Birth without sexual partnership, or parthenogenesis, is known in nature. It is not understood why some creatures, such as water-fleas and rotifer, reproduce their kind without male and female, while others do not. (Prof. John Maynard-Smith, *Daily Telegraph*, June 4, 1990). Nonetheless, the birth of Christ was supernatural, very different from any natural parthenogenesis.

# THE BLOOD OF GOD

Even greater things are revealed. The Bible declares that CHRIST's BLOOD IS ACTUALLY THE BLOOD OF GOD. Acts 20:28 speaks of *the church of God, which He purchased with his own blood.* How can that be, seeing that *God is Spirit* (John 4:24)? A spirit has no flesh and blood.

The answer is very simple:

> *The Word became flesh and dwelt among us.* (John 1:14)

In the womb of the virgin Mary, Godhood and manhood became one. The blood of Jesus is the blood of God the Son. It is divine blood. It is the blood of the Almighty, and it is all efficacious.

One individual's blood may legally be shed for one other man. But the blood of Jesus Christ has no such limitation. God's infinity is involved. The blood of the Son of God has 'grace to cover all my sin,' and the sin of the whole world.

God demonstrated the enormous capacity of the blood when Israel left Egypt. The Israelites had to slay and eat the Passover lamb. If a family was too small, they could share the lamb with another family (Exodus 12:4).

This is a lovely picture of Jesus, the Lamb of God too great for one household – for the house of Judas Iscariot, who handed Jesus as a lamb to the priests, and for the apostles at the Last Supper. One of them probably had this in mind when he wrote:

> *And He Himself is the propitiation for our sins, and not for ours only but also for the whole world.* (1 John 2:2)

Later, in visions, John saw *a great multitude which no one could number, of all nations ... [who] washed their robes and made them white in the blood of the Lamb* (Revelation 7:9, 14).

## BLOOD THAT SPEAKS

Hebrews 12:24 says that the blood of Jesus Christ is, *the blood of sprinkling that speaks better things than that of Abel.* What better word? Abel was murdered by his brother, Cain. What did his blood say, and what does the blood of Jesus Christ say?

> *The voice of your brother's blood cries out to Me from the ground. So now you [Cain] are cursed from the earth, which has opened its mouth to receive your brother's blood from your hand.* (Genesis 4:10-11)

Abel's blood cried out death and murder, and called for revenge.

The blood of Christ also discolored the dust. But what better words does it say? It speaks LIFE, not death! Abel's blood is death-blood, but the blood of Jesus is life-blood. Abel's blood called for revenge, but the blood of Jesus speaks FORGIVENESS.

Charles Wesley wrote:

> Five bleeding wounds He bears,
> Received on Calvary;
> They pour effectual prayers,
> They strongly plead for me;
> 'Forgive him, O forgive,' they cry,
> 'Nor let that ransomed sinner die.'

Cain was punished for Abel's death, but nobody suffered for Christ's death. Instead, Christ suffered death for us. No blood feud began at Calvary. The assassination of the Archduke Ferdinand started World War I, but Christ *made peace through the blood of His cross* (Colossians 1:20).

When soldiers used hammer and nails to spike Jesus Christ's living flesh to the timber gallows, His blood splashed them. They literally had the blood of Christ on their hands. Yet Jesus kept on praying, *"Father, forgive them, for they do not know what they do"* (Luke 23:34). If God forgave the sin of those soldiers it was only by the same blood, which they caused to flow. *Without shedding of blood there is no remission* (Hebrews 9:22), and that only by the blood of Jesus Christ.

## LIFE BLOOD

The blood of Jesus brings LIFE. He said so himself:

> *Whoever eats My flesh and drinks My blood has eternal life, and I will raise him up at the last day.* (John 6:54)

'Drinking' is, of course, a figure of speech, not literal, for Jesus was still alive when He spoke these words. It means taking God's forgiveness through the blood of Jesus by faith, and spiritually applying His blood to our need.

Now the true heights of Calvary's mountain soar before us. When the spear opened the heart of Jesus and blood and water came forth, the heart of God was opened too. When life-streams flowed on the Cross, an eternal fountain of life and mercy began.

Still it flows as fresh as ever,
From my Savior's wounded side.

## NOT WATER, BUT BLOOD

After Abel's murder defiled the ground, as recorded in Genesis 4:11, another killing, by Lamech, is recorded in verses 21-24. The weapon forged by Tubal-Cain and the wicked deed, glorified in music by Jubal, prompted more and more bloodshed. Abel's blood that had cried in solo from the earth swelled to a mighty choir of voices, and God heard. We read that finally *the earth also was corrupt before God, and the earth was filled with violence* (Genesis 6:11). So God declared, *"I Myself am bringing floodwaters on the earth"* (Genesis 6:17). God called Noah into the Ark, and *all the fountains of the great deep were broken up, and the windows of heaven were opened* (Genesis 7:11).

Swirling waters covered the earth to the mountain tops. Was the earth washed clean? Indeed not. Immediately after the Flood, God told Noah that only blood could cleanse sin. God had much to teach mankind:

> *Whoever sheds man's blood, by man his blood shall be shed.* (Genesis 9:6)

There was only one way:

> *Behold! The Lamb of God who takes away the sin of the world!* (John 1:29)

> *The blood of Jesus Christ His Son cleanses us from all sin.* (1 John 1:7)

His blood removes it all. Some people think that the waters of baptism can cleanse their souls. As they pass through the waters, they imagine that the religious ceremony has taken their sin away. But it simply cannot do that. If the waters of baptism could remove our sin, Jesus Christ would never have needed to die such a cruel death – but there was no alternative.

## BOUGHT BACK

The Bible speaks of our being *redeemed ... with the precious blood of Christ* (1 Peter 1:18-19), which means that we were 'bought back' by Jesus. By following Satan and sin, man sold himself to the devil and had to be redeemed. When Jesus paid for our redemption with His precious blood, does that mean that the blood was paid to Satan? No, definitely not!

The price for our salvation was paid into the court of God's justice, as Hebrews 9:24-26 indicates. The Lord paid the full price. The divine currency for our salvation was not in His pocket, but flowed in His veins! There was no question of negotiation, discount, rebate, or bargaining! Jesus gave the last drop of His heart's blood for us. Therefore our salvation cannot be challenged by anyone on earth, in heaven or under the earth, not in time nor in eternity!

# THE MARK OF THE BLOOD: INTERNAL, EXTERNAL, ETERNAL

I can now explain one of the most thrilling, often overlooked truths about the blood of Jesus. It marks those who trust in Jesus Christ, and distinguishes them from everybody else.

1. The first mark is INTERNAL, the sign of inner cleansing. When a sinner calls on the name of the Lord to be saved, and takes Jesus Christ personally as his Savior, the blood of Jesus does a deep and thorough work. We are clean in soul and mind, conscious, subconscious, or unconscious. Every evil image is thrown down. No more nightmares about hell and judgment, but divine visions and dreams. It is wonderful to dream about Jesus. Our past has gone and God remembers it no more. There is no need to keep digging it up and asking again for forgiveness. God never recalls it. This, however, does not mean that we are already spiritually perfected Christians. As we feed on the Word of God, the Holy Spirit will lead us from dimension to dimension.

2. The next mark is EXTERNAL. I can explain it through the Bible; it was foreshadowed in the Old Testament and fulfilled in the New Testament. In the Old Testament we read:

> *Moses killed* [the ram]. *Also he took some of its blood and put it on the tip of Aaron's right ear, on the thumb of his right hand, and on the big toe of his right foot.* (Leviticus 8:23)

This is the New Testament fulfillment: After Jesus has cleansed us inwardly from all our sins by His blood, an outward mark is impressed upon us. Just as there was one drop of blood upon the right ear, on the thumb and on the big toe, so the born-again believer is blood-marked.

Of course, this is not a sign on our physical body, but one that both heaven and hell can discern. Satan sees it. When God's people walk through the streets the demons can spot them. I imagine one evil spirit calling to another, "Can you see over there? That one has the blood-mark of Jesus on his ear, toe and thumb. He belongs to Jesus Christ! Don't try to touch him — it's too dangerous. Dare to touch him and you will have a legion of angels to contend with."

> *As long as we follow Him, He will not allow repossession of His property by unclean spirits.*

We human beings look after our property and protect it. You can be absolutely sure that God looks after His property too. We cost God too much for Him to neglect and lose us. We were *bought at a price,* even the precious blood of Jesus (1 Corinthians 6:20). When Jesus takes over, He saves and keeps us. As long as we follow Him, He will not allow repossession of His property by unclean spirits.

> *He who dwells in the secret place of the Most High shall abide under the shadow of the Almighty.* (Psalm 91:1)

> *And they overcame him by the blood of the Lamb and by the word of their testimony, and they did not love their lives to the death.* (Revelation 12:11)

This is the glorious and perfect protection that the Lord gives His children, free of charge.

> *No weapon formed against you shall prosper, and every tongue which rises against you in judgment you shall condemn. This is the heritage of the servants of the Lord, and their righteousness is from Me,"* says the Lord. (Isaiah 54:17)

No curse can be fastened on you, and no witchcraft can harm you. *Like a flitting sparrow, like a flying swallow, so a curse without cause shall not alight* (Proverbs 26:2).

We serve an Almighty God, not a struggling God, who might sometimes lose battles. He cannot be blackmailed nor forced to compromise with the devil. He could never go into partnership and share His right of possession of you with any evil spirit. Follow Jesus and you are wholly the Lord's. Reinhard Bonnke lives with this assurance – I am marked by the blood of Jesus, and nobody can pluck me from His hand. Satan cannot kidnap my soul. It is hidden with Christ in God, which is a safe in a strongroom, and bears the seal-mark of the blood (Colossians 3:3).

> *We serve an Almighty God, not a struggling God who might sometimes lose battles.*

3. The third mark is ETERNAL. The blood mark stays there. It does not rub off. It outlasts time. We need to appreciate our salvation though, and keep on following Jesus. The blood of Jesus is no license to sin. But God has given us everlasting salvation, and we are His forever, not just when we feel well. Hallelujah! All heaven will be filled with the blood marked saints, and not one will be in hell – not even by accident.

## THE MOUSE THAT ROARED

Somebody said that the blood of Jesus has 'reduced the devil.' The Bible says that he is *like a roaring lion* (1 Peter 5:8). He comes in the darkness and tries to frighten the children of God with his mighty roar. But when you switch on the light of the Word of God, you discover that there is no lion. There is only a mouse with a microphone!

John Bunyan said the lion at the side of the path has neither fangs nor claws. Christ pulled them out at Calvary. *He shall bruise your head, and you shall bruise His heel* (Genesis 3:15). And at Calvary it happened: That nailed-down foot of Jesus somehow came down on Satan's head – and crushed it. Since that moment the devil has suffered some kind of 'brain-damage.' He can no more think the things of God (Matthew 16:23). In the Garden of Eden God already knew that the blood of His mighty Son would destroy the works of the devil.

It was no empty promise that Jesus gave His disciples, which includes you and me:

> *He gave them power over unclean spirits, to cast them out,*
> *and to heal all kinds of sickness and all kinds of disease.*
> (Matthew 10:1)

Jesus could do that because He has power over the devil.

Jesus' power leaves nothing untouched: body, soul, mind, spirit, heart. It reaches right to the depths of our being. His blood is the secret of victory. Let Jesus mark you, INTERNALLY, EXTERNALLY, ETERNALLY, and you will be a son or daughter of God, a member of the royal house of the Lord.

## WHAT YOU SHOULD DO NOW!

Jesus said in John 6:37, *"All that the Father gives Me will come to Me, and the one who comes to Me I will by no means cast out."* This includes you, wherever and whoever you are. When you repeat the following prayer from the bottom of your heart, God will hear and answer, and save you on the spot.

*Dear heavenly Father,*

*I come to You in the name of Jesus Christ.*

*I come with all my sins, burdens, and addictions.*

*Wash me now with the precious blood of Jesus shed on Calvary.*

*Break the chains of sin and Satan in my life and family.*

*Mark me with Your precious blood externally.*

*I want to be Yours, spirit, soul, and body, for my time on earth and in eternity.*

*I put my faith in You alone, Lord Jesus Christ.*

*You are the Son of the living God.*

*I believe with my heart what I now confess with my mouth:*

*You are my Savior, Lord, and God.*

*Now I am born again — a child of God.*

*I believe it and I receive it in the name of Jesus.*

*Amen.*

❧

# THE HOLY SPIRIT BAPTISM

# THE HOLY SPIRIT BAPTISM

## WHAT IS IT?

### THE EDICT

The most wonderful sound ever heard was about to fall on the ears of the tens of thousands of people gathered in the Temple courts at Jerusalem. The final rituals of a national festival were taking place. All eyes followed a golden pitcher filled with water and wine. A drink offering was ready to be poured out to the Lord.

A priest lifted the gleaming vessel in the sunshine and paused. Silence fell as the people strained to hear the sacred water splashing into a bronze bowl at the altar.

Then came the interruption: a voice not known for a thousand years – a voice that made the spine tingle. It was the voice of Jesus Christ, the Son of God. He was the Word who had spoken in the beginning and called forth heaven and earth into existence. Now at Jerusalem, He stood and issued a royal and divine edict, changing the dispensation of God:

> *If anyone thirsts, let him come to Me and drink. He who believes in Me, as the Scripture has said, out of his heart will flow rivers of living water.* (John 7:37-38)

## STREAMS IN THE DESERT

*Rivers of living water*! Not bottles, but rivers – fresh, lively, sparkling, abundant, unending.

Some people live for what comes out of a bottle. The world's supermarkets have very little that is fresh. Pre-packed pleasure is big business, with canned music, films, records, books. Television provides the highlights of life for millions of people, just watching others live or pretending to live, even for children, who forget how to play.

People are always 'going to live' ... after things change, after working hours, when they have money, when they get married, retire or go on holiday. Jesus came to give us life NOW. NO WAITING, wherever we are, whatever we are doing. He makes us alive.

> *Jesus came to give us life NOW!*
> *No waiting, wherever we are, whatever we are doing. He makes us alive.*

God wrote His plan for Israel in the wilderness across a blackboard forty years wide. The Israelites did not have to drink stale, flat water from skins. The Lord opened bubbling streams from a rock (Exodus 17:1-7). The Temple drink offering was a celebration in memory of that wilderness water (Numbers 20:1-13). Jesus, however, gave it a new and glorious meaning, a symbol of the outpouring of the Holy Spirit.

## ONLY JESUS

This Jesus! Nobody else had ever dared make such an amazing claim – and fulfill it. He would ascend to glory where Creation began and change the order of things. Something not known before would surge from heaven to earth. He called it *The Promise of the Father* (Acts 1:4). *The* promise. Out of over eight thousand promises in God's Word, the designation of *'the promise'* makes it stand singularly and significantly alone. Christ made it His own promise. The Father's gift to Him is His gift to us, as John the Baptist said:

> *I did not know Him, but He who sent me to baptize with water said to me, 'Upon whom you see the Spirit descending, and remaining on Him, this is He who baptizes with the Holy Spirit.' And I have seen and testified that this is the Son of God.* (John 1:33-34)

## WHEN WORDS FAIL

John used a different expression here instead of *"rivers of living water."* Scripture has many other terms, such as:

> Being *baptized with fire* (Matthew 3:11, Luke 3:16); *endued with power* (Luke 24:49); anointed with the oil of God; immersed in the Spirit; *filled with the Spirit* (Ephesians 5:18); walking, praying, living in the Spirit (Galatians 5:25, Romans 8:26); our body is *the temple of the Holy Spirit* (1 Corinthians 6:19); having *another Helper* besides Christ Himself (John 14:16).

These are sketches, but color and details have to be added. The Bible is a picture gallery of the Holy Spirit in operation; it portrays signs, wonders and miracles. Men looking *as if they had been with Jesus.* The world turned upside down. People coming to *know the Lord,* enjoying a new experience. Not just religious enthusiasts, churchgoers, but a new breed with vibrant faith. Paul says that God, *even when we were dead in trespasses, made us alive together with Christ* (Ephesians 2:5) and that we are *strengthened with all might, according to His glorious power* (Colossians 1:11). The Lord Jesus Christ Himself promised it: *You shall receive power when the Holy Spirit has come upon you* (Acts 1:8).

We as born-again believers are special; we are saints, and the baptism in the Spirit is Christ's next major experience for us. Jesus alone made it possible when He died and rose and sat down at the right hand of the Majesty on High. What a gift!

## WHO IS THE HOLY SPIRIT?

The Lord does not send publicity by heavenly mail to tell us who He is. The works performed by His Spirit are seen on earth. *The Holy Spirit is a Person; He is God in action.* Creation came as *the Spirit of God was hovering over the face of the waters* (Genesis 1:2). Then, when God chose His servants, the power of the Holy Spirit rested upon them:

> *See, the Lord has called by name Bezalel ... and He has filled him with the Spirit of God, in wisdom and understanding, in knowledge and all manner of workmanship ... He has put in his heart the ability to teach, in him and Aholiab.* (Exodus 35:30-31, 34)
>
> *The spirit of the Lord came upon him* [Othniel], *and he judged Israel.* (Judges 3:10)
>
> *But the Spirit of the Lord came upon Gideon; then he blew the trumpet, and the Abiezrites gathered behind him.* (Judges 6:34)

The Spirit 'clothed Gideon with Himself' is the meaning of the above Judges 6:34, and Gideon defended Israel (Judges 6:11 – 8:35). The Spirit moved Samson to acts of supernormal strength (Judges 13 – 16:31). The Spirit of the Lord came upon Jephtha and delivered Israel's foes into his hands (Judges 11 – 12:7).

After these judges the prophet Samuel guided an entire nation for a life-time. How? *Holy men of God spoke as they were moved by the Holy Spirit* (2 Peter 1:21). The prophet Micah testified, *"truly I am full of power by the Spirit of the Lord"* (Micah 3:8).

These are portraits of the Holy Spirit. This is the Spirit that Christ promised – the Spirit of wisdom and knowledge; creative, empowering, healing; the Spirit of strength, confidence and virtue.

God's power is not a kind of supercharge for people already gifted with great personality and drive, but is for those who need it, the weak and the unknown. *He gives power to the weak, and to those who have no might He increases strength* (Isaiah 40:29).

## FOUR GREAT PICTURES

Four of the pictures in the Bible gallery should be examined carefully.

**The first picture:** Moses put his hands on seventy elders at the Tent of Meeting, and the Spirit of God came upon them. At that moment back in the camp, Eldad and Medad were also endued, and began to prophesy. A young man ran to tell Moses. Joshua thought Moses should have a monopoly on prophesying and urged, *"Moses my lord, forbid them!"* Far from objecting, Moses said, *"Are you zealous for my sake? Oh, that all the Lord's people were prophets and that the Lord would put His Spirit upon them"* (Numbers 11:24-29).

Seventy at once! That was the most for over twelve hundred years. The experience was rare, usually temporary and only for individuals. However, Moses' wish lay in many hearts while long centuries passed.

**The second picture:** The Temple that Solomon had built was in full operation, but sin had weakened the nation. A prophet stood in

Jerusalem, bringing a warning of judgment. Through the telescope of prophecy Joel had seen distant skies black with war clouds, terror and destruction, Israel laid waste – which, as we now know, proved Joel to be a true prophet. However, Joel was telling Israel more. Beyond the gathering storm, he saw bright skies, not merely recovery, but a wonderful New Thing.

> *And it shall come to pass afterward that I will pour out My Spirit on all flesh; your sons and your daughters shall prophesy, your old men shall dream dreams, your young men shall see visions. And also on My menservants and on My maidservants I will pour out My Spirit in those days.* (Joel 2:28-30)

In those days, young slave girls poured water on the hands of their mistresses to wash them, but God promised to pour out His Spirit even on them. In fact, it meant that the HOLY SPIRIT WOULD BE POURED OUT WORLDWIDE UPON ALL MANNER OF PEOPLE.

This was sensational. What He had once granted to only a handful of His chosen servants would be a privilege everyone could call his own. It was too hard for many to imagine or believe. But God said it, and His Word stands forever.

**The third picture:** John the Baptist in leather clothing stood on the bank of the Jordan River. He was the first prophet of God in four hundred years. Crowds came out to hear him and be baptized. His thunderous message called on Israel to repent and prepare because the long-awaited Coming One would appear.

> *I indeed baptize you with water unto repentance, but He who is coming after me is mightier than I, whose sandals I am not worthy to carry. He will baptize you with the Holy Spirit and fire.* (Matthew 3:11)

Twenty-four hours later, among the candidates for baptism, John saw a young man wading through the waters and stood aghast: "You! Jesus! I am not worthy to baptize you. You should baptize me!" God had shown John that Jesus was that promised *Coming One* (Matthew 11:3, Luke 7:19-20). He would perform a rite far greater than John in the Jordan. Jesus the Baptizer would not use a physical element, water, but heavenly fire, which is a spiritual element. John stood in the cold waters of the Jordan, but Jesus stood in a river of liquid fire. John had baptized for a few short days; Jesus would baptize down through the ages, not just one group on the day of Pentecost, but *all flesh*. He is doing so even now, some seven hundred and twenty thousand days later!

**The fourth picture**: Fearing the authorities who had executed Jesus, one hundred and twenty disciples came together quietly. Jesus had said, *"tarry in the city of Jerusalem until you are endued with power from on high"* (Luke 24:49). They sat and waited, and the world forgot them. Nothing happened; no marvels occurred; everything seemed so ordinary.

The tenth day was a Sunday, the Feast of Weeks, also called Pentecost. At nine in the morning, a Temple priest lifted the bread of the firstfruits and waved it before the Lord. As if this were a signal for the ascended Christ, a divine tornado tore through the skies above Jerusalem.

Jesus Himself had broken through the heavens in His shattering and victorious **Ascension**. Now through the opened skies there was a **Descension**. The Holy Spirit came, demonstrating that the way into the heavenlies was open. Praise God, it has never been closed since! When the curtain of the Temple was ripped as Jesus died, the priests probably tried to stitch it together again. Nobody can stitch up this rent in the heavens, not even the devil and all his minions. It is a new and living way, open forever.

Moses saw God as fire in the bush. Now through this door of glory, which no man could shut, the same fire, the Holy Spirit, came. Amber flames settled in burning beauty upon the head of each waiting disciple. Glory that filled all heaven now crowded into the breasts of those present. The Holy Spirit was in them and on them. Men had never experienced it before. There were no words to describe it. This was unutterable. Then God gave them words, new tongues and languages to tell *"the wonderful works of God"* (Acts 2:11) like inspired psalmists.

*Amber flames settled in burning beauty upon the head of each waiting disciple.*

## THE BAPTISM AND OTHER WORKINGS

We receive salvation and are born again through the Holy Spirit. But that is not the end of His work. His activities are manifold. He empowers us for witnessing in particular. The baptism in the Spirit means that people saved by grace and born again can have new experiences and become Spirit-energized witnesses for Christ.

How necessary this is! It was vital even for the disciples who had healed the sick and cast out demons. That was possible only as long as Christ was by their sides. The Lord Jesus told them to wait until they were endued with the Spirit before they went forth into the fields for service. Mary the mother of Christ was one example. She had certainly known the Holy Spirit in her life to bring about the birth of Jesus, but she too waited at Jerusalem for this further work of the Spirit, called *the Promise of the Father* (Acts 1:4). If she needed it, we all do.

The explanation is simple: The disciples belonged to Christ. He said so, and as long as He was with them on earth, they could do marvelous works. Then He ascended to God, and they felt lonely and frightened. However, the Lord had made a promise: He would send *another Helper*, that is, the Holy Spirit (John 14:16).

The word 'Helper' suggests someone readily available to give assistance when necessary. Jesus had been by their sides for over three years, and He was their first great Helper, Companion, and Comforter. Then that other Person, another Helper, the Holy Spirit, came on the Day of Pentecost. It was like having Jesus with them again, and they were able to carry out the Great Commission to preach the Gospel, heal the sick, cast out devils and work wonders as before – in short, the work of witnessing, which is the privilege and responsibility of every born again person (Matthew 28:19-20, Mark 16:15-18).

> *When Christ baptizes us in the Spirit, we partake of the character of the Holy Spirit.*

The same situation exists for us. First, we must come to Christ and give ourselves to Him, and then receive the power baptism. Our very lives should be evidence of His Resurrection. It is more than talk that is needed – it is people manifesting the fullness of the Spirit.

The word 'baptism' did not have a religious meaning originally. It is from the trade of dyeing fabrics. The English equivalent is 'dipping.' The cloth or garment is dipped into the dye, and the cloth takes on the color or character of the dye. When Christ baptizes us in the Spirit, we partake of the 'color' or character of the Spirit, *partakers of the divine nature* (2 Peter 1:4). The Spirit is in us, and we in the Spirit. We are people of the Holy Spirit.

It was not just seeing Jesus, or hearing His voice which made the disciples the great people they were, because some believed *but some doubted* (Matthew 28:17; Mark 16:13-14: Luke 24:41), but it was the Holy Spirit baptism. They shut the door when they met for fear of the Jews (John 20:19). They certainly did not shout in the streets, "Jesus is alive!" They met secretly, at first away in Galilee, and they even went fishing (John 21:3). All that changed, however, on the Day of Pentecost. Instead of being afraid of the Jewish crowds, the crowds now trembled before them and cried out, *"Men and brethren, what shall we do?"* (Acts 2:37) This was as Jesus said:

> *But you shall receive power when the Holy Spirit has come upon you; and you shall be witnesses to Me ... to the end of the earth.* (Acts 1:8)

## HOW IT FIRST HAPPENED

Now we look again at the fourth picture:

> *When the Day of Pentecost had fully come, they were all with one accord in one place. And suddenly there came a sound from heaven, as of a rushing mighty wind, and it filled the whole house where they were sitting. Then there appeared to them divided tongues, as of fire, and one sat upon each of them. And they were all filled with the Holy Spirit and began to speak with other tongues, as the ¡Spirit gave them utterance.* (Acts 2:1-4)

What divine power and glory! This second chapter of Acts is noisy and action-packed. The heavenly Father does not make empty promises, just to build up our hopes and then laugh at us. Christ had said, *"Go into all the world"* (Mark 16:15). The moment those tongues of fire touched their heads, it put the 'go' into them. God acted and then they acted. Divine action caused human reaction, which is why this book is called the "Acts of the Apostles."

There was an inflow from heaven, and there had to be an outflow. *Out of his heart will flow rivers of living water* (John 7:38), not just 'into.'

It was not for emotional satisfaction. The disciples did not say, "Let us have a prayer meeting for power like this every week." They never again asked for power for themselves, because they knew that they had it already. The apostle Peter said to the cripple at the Gate Beautiful, "*What I do have, I give you*" (Acts 3:6, emphasis added).

> *Never again did the disciples ask for power for themselves, because they knew that they already had it!*

Nor did they just sit, appointing a chairman and passing resolutions on social problems. They could not contain themselves! They had to be up and doing. Peter stood, electrified, and the Christian age began; the world heard the first Gospel sermon.

The result? Three thousand people received salvation. That was the reason for Pentecost. In fact, the Trinity, the whole Godhead, set the plans of salvation and evangelism into motion. The Father joined with the ascended Lord to send the Spirit to save a lost world (Isaiah 48:16). That is the main purpose of the baptism in the Spirit. That is what God is doing: saving people. What are we doing? This baptism is not for thrills, but to help us work alongside the Lord. We know why Jesus and the Holy Spirit came. Why are we here?

What a day Pentecost was! 'Rivers' flowed that eventually flooded the Roman Empire. People sigh and wish they were back in the days of the early Church, but it was neither the days, nor the men, which made the time special. It was the baptism in the Holy Spirit. Without it, the disciples would probably have gone back to being fishermen in Galilee, and grown old telling tales of strange events when they were young. Instead, they changed the world. THAT BAPTISM IS FOR ALL TODAY.

# FOR TODAY

Some people want to deprive believers today, saying the baptism in the Spirit with signs following was only for the first believers, "until the Church got under way." They suggest that we have to manage without the miraculous gifts of those believers. That would make the early Christians an elite group, as if we could not be Christians in the way they were. However, not a word in the Bible suggests such a thing. It is a theory invented by unbelief. In fact, when Paul went to Ephesus twenty years after the Church had been well planted, twelve people were baptized in the Spirit (Acts 19:6-7).

Every generation needs Pentecost. In A.D. 30 the world population was one hundred million. Today, it is six billion and growing rapidly. Ten times more people today than in the first century do not know about Jesus. The Church still needs planting. Unbelief and complete ignorance of God exist everywhere. Surely our need for the power of the Holy Spirit is far more desperate.

Therefore, I want to explain to you carefully, from the Bible itself, why and how that same baptism is for us today. Read what Peter preached to the multitude on the Day of Pentecost, under the anointing of the Spirit, when he explained who could be baptized in the Holy Spirit:

> *For the promise is to you and to your children, and to all who are afar off, as many as the Lord our God will call.* (Acts 2:39)

**First**, Peter said it is to you, the very people he had just accused saying, "*Him* [Jesus] *you have taken by lawless hands, have crucified, and put to death*" (Acts 2:23). Yet he announced:

*Repent, and let every one of you be baptized in the name of
Jesus Christ for the remission of sins; and you shall receive
the gift of the Holy Spirit.* (Acts 2:38)

These were the same people that Jesus had called *an evil generation*
(Luke 11:29) and *faithless and perverse* (Matthew 17:17; Luke 9:41).

**Second**, he said it is *to your children* – the next generation.
Some people would not become parents until later. It could be
that one hundred years after the Day of Pentecost people would
receive this blessing and speak in tongues. One woman, mentioned
in Luke 2:36, had been a widow for eighty-four years. However, the
word 'children' referred not only to their families, but also to their
descendants, that is, the children of Israel.

**Third**, Peter said, "*To all that are far off.*" That is in time and distance,
to the ends of the earth where Christ had commissioned His Church
to take the Gospel (Matthew 28:19-20, Mark 16:15-16). This would
take many years, far beyond the apostolic age. For example, New
Zealand would be one of the ends of the earth, yet no missionary
arrived there until 1814. Indeed, the task is not completed even today;
therefore, we still need that same power.

**Fourth**, Peter hammered it home, *as many as the Lord our God
will call.* Those 'God calls' are those who come to Christ. *No one
can come to Me unless the Father who sent Me draws him* (John 6:44).
All believers are called, and are promised the same gift of the Holy
Spirit that Peter and his one hundred and nineteen friends had
just received. Do what the disciples did, and you will get what the
disciples got. Believe God's promises given to us all. *Do not be drunk
with wine ... but be filled with the Spirit* (Ephesians 5:18).

Only Jesus is the Baptizer, nobody else. Do not settle for a
secondhand experience. Have your own Pentecost. Do not try to
cash in on someone else's experience during a charismatic meeting.

The fire of the Holy Spirit did not arrive in one big, general flame so that all could gather and warm themselves, conducting cozy conferences. Rather, it came in separate tongues, little flames that *sat upon each of them* (Acts 2:3). This was very significant: Those tongues of fire were in fact potent and portable power stations which would move with the people wherever they went.

We live in a spiritually dark and cold world. The best way not to freeze is to be aglow with the Holy Spirit. God will light a fire on the altar of your own heart so that you can be a fire-lighter. Warm others, do not depend on others to warm you!

# THE HOLY SPIRIT BAPTISM

## HOW TO RECEIVE IT

### BELIEVING THE GIVER

Thousands of people come into our campaign meetings as unbelievers. Some of them are really far away from God: wicked, immoral, addicted, bound by the occult or working hard for religions that do nothing for them. They must first receive salvation. Paul said to converts in his day, *"you were washed, you were sanctified, you were justified in the name of the Lord Jesus and by the Spirit of our God"* (1 Corinthians 6:11). Perhaps unclean spirits had previously occupied their bodies. Yet we see hundreds of thousands of such people become temples of the Holy Spirit. How? There are only two conditions: one, *repentance*, and two, *faith* in the Lord Jesus Christ.

> *There are only two conditions: one, repentance, and two, faith in the Lord Jesus Christ.*

### REPENTANCE

Jesus said:

> *And I will pray the Father, and He will give you another Helper, that He may abide with you forever, the Spirit of truth, whom the world cannot receive, because it neither sees Him nor knows Him; but you know Him, for He dwells with you and will be in you.* (John 14:16-17)

Peter said:

> *Repent therefore and be converted, that your sins may be*
> *blotted out, so that times of refreshing may come from*
> *the presence of the Lord. Repent ... for the remission*
> *of sins; and you shall receive the gift of the Holy Spirit.*
> (Acts 3:19; 2:38)

The Holy Spirit is a most holy Being. The Bible uses the image of a
dove for the Holy Spirit. A dove is a clean bird; it will not build its
nest on a dunghill. The Holy Spirit will not settle in a sinful life;
He is too sensitive. Heavenly waters do not flow through polluted
channels, through neither foul minds nor foul mouths.

The Holy Spirit is only for the blood-washed sons and daughters of God.
Nobody can be good enough until cleansed in Calvary's fountain.
Blood comes before fire. No other cleansing is necessary or possible.
We cannot make ourselves more holy or more worthy than the
blood of Jesus already makes us. The Holy Spirit is a gift and cannot
be earned.

## FAITH

> *Without faith it is impossible to please Him, for he who comes*
> *to God must believe that He is, and that He is a rewarder*
> *of those who diligently seek Him.* (Hebrews 11:6)

> *But this He spoke concerning the Spirit, whom those*
> *believing in Him would receive; for the Holy Spirit was not*
> *yet given, because Jesus was not yet glorified.* (John 7:39)

> *O foolish Galatians! Did you receive the Spirit by the works*
> *of the law, or by the hearing of faith?* (Galatians 3:1-2)

To come to Jesus begging and pleading is not having faith at all.
FAITH INVOLVES TAKING. You do not need to persuade Jesus Christ

to be kind and baptize you in His holy fire. He has already promised. Come with boldness to collect what He is offering you. It is a gift, and you must believe the Giver before you reach out to receive what the Giver is giving.

*To come to Jesus begging and pleading is not having faith at all.*

What about 'tarrying in Jerusalem'? Jesus told the disciples to wait, *for the Holy Spirit was not yet given, because Jesus was not yet glorified* (John 7:39). They had to wait for the historic moment. But NOW HE IS HERE. Pentecost is a fact and you can experience it personally. We have no pleading meetings, only receiving meetings. Jesus loves to fulfill His Word in our lives. We are believers, not beggars.

## THE HOLY LANGUAGE

When we receive the original baptism with the Spirit, the original signs will follow.

> *And they were all filled with the Holy Spirit and began to speak with other tongues, as the Spirit gave them utterance.*
> (Acts 2:4)

How? The one hundred and twenty disciples were praising the Lord. Then came the sound of *a rushing mighty wind* (Acts 2:2) and the tongues of fire, and their hearts exploded with joy. They opened their mouths to speak, and the Spirit gave them utterance in languages unknown to them. Just like that.

If we receive the same baptism, it must have the same effect. Jesus the Baptizer has not changed, nor have His methods. In God's kingdom we are not copies of copies, but originals from The Original – JESUS CHRIST. When we experience the baptism in the Holy Spirit, we do not receive leftovers, but the original experience.

The ability to speak in tongues is mentioned throughout the book of Acts:

> And those of the circumcision who believed were astonished, as many as came with Peter, because the gift of the Holy Spirit had been poured out on the Gentiles also. (Acts 10:45-46)

Speaking in tongues was taken by the apostle Paul as evidence of the baptism in the Holy Spirit. Simon the Sorcerer 'saw' the supernatural manifestation of the Spirit (Acts 8:17-19). Paul received the baptism (Acts 9:17) and said he spoke with tongues (1 Corinthians 14:18). On other occasions, the same thing is reported (Acts 11:17, 13:52, 19:6).

> *Speaking in tongues was taken by the apostle Paul as evidence of the baptism in the Holy Spirit.*

On the Day of Pentecost, Peter explained what was happening by quoting Joel (Acts 2:17-19). Joel had prophesied that people would prophesy. When they spoke with tongues, Peter said, *This is that* ... (Acts 2:16). Speaking with tongues, when interpreted, is prophecy.

What better sign could God give to make us confident that the Holy Spirit is within and upon us as we go out to preach the Gospel? When we feel weak and fearful and hard-pressed as Paul did (1 Corinthians 2:3), the wonder of tongues assures us. Without some outward manifestation we could pray forever without being sure, and that is exactly what has happened.

What a wonderful thing! Paul described speaking in tongues as telling secrets to God (1 Corinthians 14:2). Tongues is the only language the devil cannot understand. The arch-confuser is totally confused himself, because he does not even know the alphabet of the Holy Spirit. Satan cannot crack the Holy Spirit's secret code that puts us in touch with the throne of heaven.

Our body is *the temple of the Holy Spirit* (1 Corinthians 6:19). Jesus said a temple was a house of prayer (Matthew 21:13, Mark 11:17). If our bodies are temples, houses of prayer in which the Spirit dwells, then He will pray through us, pure and powerful prayers, reaching the throne of God. The Spirit loves to pray, and that is why the Spirit-filled are eager to pray. It is not a grievous duty but a glorious pleasure and privilege. Jesus said, *"Howbeit when He, the Spirit of truth, is come, ... He shall glorify Me"* (John 16:13-14).

When Solomon dedicated the Temple, the light of the 'shekinah,' the visible glory of God, shone on the golden Mercy Seat in the Holy of Holies. After he prayed, the entire area, the Holy Place and the outside courts, was filled with the glory so that the priests could not enter, and they fell to the floor in worship and thanksgiving (2 Chronicles 7:1-3). That is an Old Testament picture.

If we are saved, the light of Christ dwells in the shrine of our inner hearts, but when we pray for the Holy Spirit, He breaks forth throughout our entire beings, spirit, soul, mind and body. He floods and baptizes our whole personalities.

## THE BAFFLED DEVIL

Finally, all you have to do is – ASK. That is all. When we are cleansed through the redeeming blood of Jesus, we are children of God. The baptism in the Holy Spirit becomes our birthright. Jesus encourages us especially about that gift: *"Ask ... seek ... knock ... for everyone who asks receives, and he who seeks finds, and to him who knocks, it will be opened"* (Luke 11:9-10). *But let him ask in faith, with no doubting* (James 1:6).

What we receive will only be from God. The devil never answers prayers prayed in the name of Jesus. He has no means of tapping our direct line to heaven if we ask the heavenly Father for the Holy Spirit. No foul demon can impersonate the Holy Spirit and come in His disguise. Read what Jesus said:

> *If a son asks for bread from any father among you, will he give him a stone? Or if he asks for a fish, will he give him a serpent instead of a fish? Or if he asks for an egg, will he offer him a scorpion?* (Luke 11:11-13)

That is the final answer. We could not have a more explicit assurance.

## WHAT YOU MUST DO NOW

Now that you have read this, you know what the Lord intends to do in your life: baptize you with the Holy Spirit. Remember that Jesus, *and Jesus alone*, is the Baptizer (John 1:33). And He is with you right now.

If you have been washed clean in the blood of the Lamb of God, then you qualify to receive this glorious gift. You need not even wait for any special church service. Jesus is with you this very moment. Begin to praise His name. Ask now! Worship the Lord, praise His name, and you will be baptized by Jesus Christ with the Holy Spirit and with fire.

What the early Christians had is as much for you as for anyone else because Jesus loves you. Remember, Jesus does not need persuading to do this. He did not need persuading to love you, and He loves you enough to baptize you with the Holy Spirit, now ... RIGHT NOW.

☙

# THE LORD YOUR HEALER

# THE LORD YOUR HEALER

## THE WHY AND HOW OF
## DIVINE HEALING

### GOD'S NATIONAL HEALTH SCHEME

Jesus Christ is the Great Physician on call day and night. His practice never closes and we do not have to wait for an appointment. He specializes in all kinds of troubles, whether sickness of the soul, afflictions of the body, or the ills of society. There are no fees.

We all enjoy good health – when we have it! Unfortunately, so many people get up in the morning feeling run down and start the day already exhausted, which was never God's idea. The Gospel of Jesus Christ is the national health scheme for every nation on earth and the Bible is its textbook. Somebody said that God meant our bodies to last, with care, a lifetime!

The first page of the Bible says that *God saw everything that He had made, and indeed it was very good* (Genesis 1:31). The last page says that *there shall be no more death, nor sorrow, nor crying. There shall be no more pain* (Revelation 21:4). Things began very well and they will end that way.

Sickness in God's good world is like weeds growing among wheat. But make no mistake – God did not sow the weeds. An enemy has done this (Matthew 13:28). God sent Jesus, *who went about doing good and healing all who were oppressed by the devil, for God was with Him* (Acts 10:38). It was the Creator's protest against the sabotage of His work by the devil.

God planted cures in nature, which medical research keeps finding. But the God who heals naturally also heals supernaturally. Scripture denies that sickness is God's will, and it credits healings to God. Today, His hand touches far more people than many realize. Throughout the world, many supernatural healings take place every year, which prove that *Jesus Christ is the same yesterday, today, and forever* (Hebrews 13:8). In our own CfaN crusades, outstanding wonders regularly take place.

# WHY WE CAN BE HEALED

### 1. We can expect healing because... Jesus never changes

Jesus healed multitudes. That was His mission. He came to heal as well as to save. He did not come from glory to earth only for those people who happened to be alive during that period in history. He did not come to bring relief merely to a few thousand people. That was only the beginning. The Bible says it was what *Jesus began both to do and teach* (Acts 1:1). By his deeds, He showed us what He wanted to do, so that we can see what He was – and still is – like. He came to heal them so that He could heal you and me.

People living in the days of Jesus' earthly ministry possibly thought of Jesus more as a Healer than anything else. He set out to heal. That was Jesus. He did not wait for the sick to come to Him – He often went to them. The apostle Peter actually said that Jesus went around for that very purpose (Acts 10:38). Healing was a major part of His mission and Jesus said God sent Him to do those very works (John 5:17, 9:3-4).

## THE PEAK OF HIS POWER

We read that *Jesus Christ is the same yesterday, today, and forever* (Hebrews 13:8). Jesus is alive, just as ready to heal now as He ever was. He is not like the moon, which has phases, sometimes showing a darkened portion. He is *The Sun of Righteousness ... with healing in His wings* (Malachi 4:2).

*From start to finish Christianity is supernatural.*

What Jesus was, He is – constantly and forever. Miracles are part and parcel of the Gospel of Jesus Christ, not something added on as an afterthought. From start to finish Christianity is supernatural, beginning as resurrection life and power. Healings demonstrate the essential truths of Christianity and show us Jesus as He really is.

Look at this Scripture:

> *Every good gift and every perfect gift is from above, and comes down from the Father of lights, with whom there is no variation or shadow of turning.* (James 1:17)

James has a picture of a sundial in mind. The sun rises and sets. As we see it move across the sky, the shadow moves across the sundial. Then comes a moment when there is no shadow. At midday the sun reaches its zenith or meridian and the shadow disappears. After miday, it begins to decline, and the shadow creeps slowly across the dial. That is what the ordinary sun does.

In contrast to the sun, James considers the *Father of lights*. Jesus Christ is the Light of all lights, the Light of the world, and there is no changing with Him causing a shadow. He is always at the peak of His power, forever at the zenith. *There is no variation or shadow of turning*. He never turns, never inclines or declines, never rises or sets. He is always at the height of His glory, pouring out His love and life in all His fullness and brilliance. That is why millions are being healed today.

If we look back, we see that what Jesus was then. He is the same today. If we look forward, we see that He will be what He was. He is not becoming great, He is great. He is now at the height of His greatness. He always was – and will always be – the Healer and the Savior.

## THE YESTERDAY, TODAY, FOREVER CHRIST

Here is an example from Luke's Gospel (7:11-16). Jesus raised a young man from the dead in the village of Nain, the son of a widow. We read that Jesus had compassion on the weeping mother. In the same region, the great prophets Elijah and Elisha had also raised mothers' sons from the dead (1 Kings 17; 2 Kings 4). That was eight hundred years before.

Now notice this. In each case, the Bible says Elijah and Elisha gave the son back to his mother. Jesus did exactly the same. He raised the young man from death, and gave him back to his mother. Christ knew the Scriptures, and it was His pointed way of showing that, what He had just done for this grieving mother, He had done long before for other mothers. It was He who had raised those two sons from death. Jesus had been around in Israel long before His birth in Bethlehem, and had worked through Elijah and Elisha. Eight centuries made no difference to His power or compassion. Generation after generation has experienced Christ's healing touch. We recognize His fingerprints, His typical way of working. He is like the noonday sun and never switches off. His powerful sunlight kills the virus of evil.

*Generation after generation has experienced Christ's healing touch.*

## 2. We can expect healing because...
## God started it

Healing originated with God. It was not our idea. At the beginning of the Bible when nobody had ever thought of such a thing, He healed people. That was four thousand years ago. *So Abraham prayed to God; and God healed Abimelech, his wife, and his female servants* (Genesis 20:17). Nobody suggested healing to God, or begged Him for it. He did it because it was His nature. He loved to do it.

If there is something you do not like doing, you keep quiet about it. If you enjoy doing something, perhaps a hobby or a sport, you devote time to it and generally talk about it, too. God did not keep quiet about healing – He could not! His heart was full of compassion. He not only talked about it, but did it as well.

> *God did not keep quiet about healing – He could not! His heart was full of compassion.*

When Jesus came He offered to heal people. We read in John's Gospel that He performed some of His miracles without being specifically asked. He went to the Pool of Bethesda where there were hundreds of afflicted people, without anybody suggesting it. He approached one paralyzed man and asked him if he wished to be healed. The man did not even say "yes," but Jesus healed him anyway (John 5). Later He saw a blind man and without even asking him what he wanted Jesus restored his sight (John 9). That is Jesus. That was Jesus yesterday, and that is Jesus today.

If a man spends seven years or more studying to become a doctor, when he has finished his studies, he will open a practice to treat sick people. It would be ridiculous for a doctor not to practice after all his efforts to qualify. We read in Matthew 8:17 that *He Himself took our infirmities and bore our sicknesses.* That is a quotation from Isaiah chapter fifty-three, about the crucifixion. Christ bore our pains and our sins in His own body on the Cross. If Jesus died for us, it is not too much to expect Him to heal us.

### 3.  We can expect healing because... of God's name

God's name is Yahweh Rapha – *I am the* LORD *who heals you.* That is like His badge of office as the Great Healer. It was given when Moses was leading Israel out of slavery. After three days passing through a waterless waste they were desperate. Then they arrived at the pool of Marah, only to find the water bitter, and undrinkable. The people were angry with Moses. There was only one thing that Moses knew he could do – cry out to God. And God performed a special wonder. He healed the bitter waters of Marah to demonstrate who He was – the Lord who heals (Exodus 15:22-26).

> *God healed the bitter waters of Marah to demonstrate who He was – the Lord who heals.*

The great span of God's goodness began to be apparent. The God who healed Marah's bitter waters would heal the foul waters of the whole world, cleansing it of bitterness. He gave us His name, Yahweh Rapha – *I am the* LORD *who heals you.* Nobody now has to draw his own conclusions about His identity. His name tells us who He is. He heals and in His glory He is doing just that. Healing is the music of His soul.

*The* LORD *who heals* was His name not exclusively for Israel, but for everybody. What God is in one place, He must always be – everywhere. *God is the King of all the earth* (Psalm 47:7). Just as I am in America or Germany, and you are you in one place or another, so the Lord is the same all over the world. God is God everywhere. There is not one kind of God in Israel and another in Europe or Africa.

Every year, He is the same God; He does not change with the seasons or the passing of the years. *I AM WHO I AM. I am the LORD who heals you. I am the LORD, I do not change* (Exodus 3:14, 15:26, Malachi 3:6). In fact, everything that God is, He always is. Everywhere, all the time, He is holy, righteous, merciful, a shepherd, the Savior, and also the healer.

## 4. We can expect healing because...
### it is in God's character to put right what is wrong

That is what the whole Bible is about – wrongs being righted, including the wrong of suffering. Scripture begins with the book of Genesis, describing the greatest of all miracles – creation. The earth was formless, dark, and empty. Then God turned it into the beautiful globe we now know. Likewise today, the Spirit of the Lord moves to transform whatever else He sees that is dark and disturbed. The desert blossoms as the rose, the rubble of bombed cities blooms with wild flowers, sinners become saints, and the sick are made whole.

When evil entered, the Garden of Eden withered. Then the Lord stepped in with His plan of redemption. He continues to work out His plan to this very day. *"My Father has been working until now, and I have been working"* said Jesus (John 5:17). Romans chapter eight promises that the whole creation will be delivered from corruption. The last book in the Bible tells us that the leaves of the tree of life will be used for *the healing of the nations* (Revelation 22:2). Healing by leaves! God does not work by brute force but by mercy. We can come to God confident of His sympathy in our physical need. Our self-curing mechanism has been broken. People are ill and God is unhappy about it.

### 5. We can expect healing because...
### God's mercies are for everybody

After Jesus had been away from Nazareth for about a year, He went back and preached in the synagogue that He had once so faithfully attended (Luke 4:16-30). In His sermon, He talked about Naaman. This man was a leper, a foreign army general from Syria who had taken some Israelite people captive. He had an Israelite slave girl. But God still healed him (2 Kings 5). Jesus also talked about a widow, similarly a foreigner. God sent Elijah to her and, during a famine, fed not only the widow and Elijah but the widow's family as well. Jesus was showing that God was concerned with people everywhere, not just the 'chosen people.'

In fact the first people to experience divine healing were Philistines. God sent them to Abraham, who would pray for them and they would be healed (Genesis 20). Abraham certainly did not trust them, and later the Philistines became Israel's enemies. But God's mercies are worldwide. He does not only heal great saints, but sinful people as well.

### 6. We can expect healing because...
### of God's promises

It would need a book to quote all the promises of God, but one quotation, which is typical, can be found in James 5:14-16: *The prayer of faith will save the sick, and the Lord will raise him up. And if he has committed sins, he will be forgiven.*

Actually, every time Christ healed someone, it was also a promise. Whatever God did, He did it to show us what He will do. The works of Jesus are prophecies and signs. To heal just a few sick individuals in the past was never His plan or wish. Some people have suggested it was, but nothing that they ever wrote is utterly convincing.

We cannot believe that of Jesus. His earthly ministry was a demonstration of what He is. It was meant to encourage our faith. Healing was a major part of Christ's ministry. We cannot write it off as having no connection with our present needs. People get sick now just as they did then. Jesus knows that this is the case, which is why we have the Gospels to tell us what He did about it. It is all there, full of significance, for our hope and comfort. It can mean only one thing – Jesus still heals today!

*Healing was a major part of Christ's ministry.*

Some people have the upside-down idea that giving testimonies about healing is wrong in case it builds up 'false hopes' in others. This is really a criticism of the Gospels, which are full of such testimonies. The stories are bound to create faith. They are surely there to do so. If you do not want to encourage people to look for healing, do not let them see the Bible! No book generates such a wealth of hope as the Bible. No preacher encouraged people like Jesus. Every Scripture testimony is like God saying, "*try Me now in this*" (Malachi 3:10).

## 7. We can expect healing because... Jesus said "I will"

In order to create trust in God, the Bible gives us story after story. The New Testament turns the spotlight first on a leper (Matthew 8:1-3). Jesus had just come down after giving His Sermon on the Mount and this victim of disease met Him. He said, "*Lord, if You are willing, You can make me clean.*" That is the crucial question for many people. Will God do what He can?

First, we all need to know that He can. God is 'the Almighty.' If He could not heal the sick, then He would not be Almighty, and thus not God. In Jeremiah 32:27 we read God's question: "*Behold, I am the LORD, the God of all flesh. Is there anything too hard for Me?*"

No answer was needed. God calls Himself *the God of all flesh.* *Therefore,* God can heal flesh.

So, He can, but will He? The story, in Matthew chapter eight, gives us the answer. *Jesus put out His hand and touched him, saying, "I am willing; be cleansed." Immediately his leprosy was cleansed.* Immediately afterwards, we see in the same chapter, a Roman centurion whose servant was ill. Jesus said, *"I will come and heal him"* (verse 7). Those two powerful words 'I will' reveal God's heart. Christ's words never pass away. His 'I will' is a cosmic law. His words are written in heaven, carved in the foundation of the world. It is God's 'Amen!' to our hopes, written into the constitution of the kingdom of God.

God says 'I will' countless times throughout the Old Testament. The words are the key to God's covenanted promises to bless the world. The first covenant (Genesis 9) shows God wanting to take care of every creature on earth – it is one big 'I will' from start to finish. Exodus is a book of God's covenant with Israel and 'I will' is used nearly one hundred times. It comes forty-six times in just six chapters of Isaiah, and nineteen times in a single chapter of Jeremiah (chapter thirty-one). When Jesus said 'I will' it gathered all God's hundreds of 'I will' promises, and focused their power like a laser beam on the leper, burning out his disease. God's 'I will' includes His will to heal.

> *God says 'I will' countless times throughout the Old Testament.*

In the matter of healing, God still says 'I will.' Somebody might say, "I was prayed for and not healed, so it is not God's will." The logic is wrong. There could be other reasons. Not being healed has nothing to do with the will of God. God does not change His mind – not just for you! You may not be healed, although it is certainly His will. God's will is not always done, which is why Christ taught us to pray, *"Your will be done."* He said that *"men always ought to pray and not lose heart"* (Luke 18:1). Many sail in such shallow waters of faith their keel grinds on the gravel all the way to glory!

## 8. We can expect healing because...
### Christ introduced the kingdom of God into this world

The kingdom of God is a kind of fourth dimension, a supernatural order with power to override the natural order. The hand of a man can make things happen that would normally not happen naturally, and so can the hand of God. Jesus brought the powers of heaven to people on earth. Christianity is miraculous.

## 9. We can expect healing for the greatest reason of all:
### Christ died for us

Here are two wonderful biblical encouragements. *He who did not spare His own Son, but delivered Him up for us all, how shall He not with Him also freely give us all things?* (Romans 8:32). *"He Himself took our infirmities and bore our sicknesses"* (Matthew 8:17). The Lord made heaven and earth. Jesus conquered death. He does not give up at the sight of a mere cripple or a cancer.

# HOW WE CAN BE HEALED

## 1. We can be healed...
### by the laying on of hands

This is the normal Scriptural pattern. Jesus said of those who follow Him, *"They will lay hands on the sick, and they will recover"* (Mark 16:18). The ordinary hands of an ordinary person bring about a miraculous change in an afflicted person. How? It is quite simple – that is the way God planned it. Mortals become retailers of His wholesale blessings. Divine power operates through 'manpower.' That is a great principle. It runs through all creation. It seems futile to bury a seed for it to die, but God brings it to life to spring up and bear fruit. It may seem futile to put our hand on a person, but that is nonetheless all God wants. It produces wonders. We plant, God gives the increase. We lay on hands, He heals. We preach – He saves.

Why did God plan it like that? *First*, God wants us to be channels of His love. He sheds His love in our hearts for us to carry it to others in a practical way. People see that God loves them, and it teaches us to serve others with love. *Second*, God wants to share His pleasure with us. He takes delight in blessing and healing and saving. If we work with Him we share that delight. He says, *"Enter into the joy of your lord"* (Matthew 25:23).

## 2. We can be healed...
## by praying when afflicted

Divine healing is part of the subject of prayer. Many thousands of people have recovered as they prayed.

God always hears your prayers. Sometimes God does not give you a direct and personal reply, but sends the answer through a human channel such as the ministry of one of His servants. The *gifts of healings* (1 Corinthians 12:9) are for that purpose. God gives healings to somebody as to a steward. That person is responsible for bringing healing to sick people who have prayed. You pray, and God sends the answer through them.

Often, I have known that I had a healing for someone who had been praying, and they have come forward in the service and received it. In one meeting in Norway, God kept saying "paralysis" to me until

I prayed for the person, unknown to me, who was suffering from this affliction. A woman at the back of the crowd had often sought God on that very matter, and that day He sent the answer. I was a bit like a dispatch rider from God. So all over the world, the vast majority of people find deliverance through the ordinance of laying on of hands, sometimes accompanied by anointing with oil (Mark 16:18, James 5:14-16). Obedience to the Word of God brings blessing.

*Obedience to the Word of God brings blessing.*

3. We can be healed...
   without doing anything about it ourselves

A woman was carried into one of our campaign meetings in a coma. By the Holy Spirit, I became aware of it. When I declared that God had whispered this information to me, He immediately touched her, and she became conscious and well. God touches children and babies, who cannot understand. He heals people too ill to think. They cannot do anything themselves, but they recover, simply by a sovereign act of God.

It is common for people to be healed without expecting it. In one of our Gospel campaigns a gang came along to cause a riot. They brought a blind man as an excuse to stir up trouble if my prayers did not heal him. While he was just standing with them, his sight was restored. On another occasion, a demented man came to a meeting and stood at the back of the crowd. Suddenly, the Lord went across to him, without my doing anything. The evil spirit left him, and the man came to himself all at once and wondered what he was doing there!

Sometimes God cannot wait for us to act. He is there to heal, and He does what He is there to do – He heals.

## 4. We can be healed...
## through other people's faith

*Is anyone among you sick? Let him call for the elders of the church, and let them pray over him ... and the prayer of faith will save the sick, and the Lord will raise him up ... pray for one another, that you may be healed.* (James 5:14-16)

In Mark 2:1-12 a man was brought to Jesus on a stretcher carried by four others. We read that *when Jesus saw their faith, He said to the paralytic ... "arise, take up your bed, and go to your house." Immediately he arose, took up the bed, and went out in the presence of them all.*

Prayers in our services have brought deliverance to people miles away who did not know they were being prayed for. Indeed, do not we all pray for absent friends, and successfully? Doctors talk about 'spontaneous' remissions. Nothing is spontaneous, there is always a cause.

The world-famous poet Alfred Lord Tennyson wrote, "More things are wrought by prayer than this world dreams of." He was right.

## 5. We can be healed...
## through our own faith

This brings us to what many see as a crucial matter. Little is said about faith in this book, because so many give up at its very mention, as if faith was too much to ask of them. Take special note – God does not do the impossible only by impossible faith. He only wants possible faith – faith that is possible for you.

The disciples asked Jesus to increase their faith. From the millions of sermons preached you would think He would do just that, but He did not! He explained that faith is not a matter of size. *If you have faith as a mustard seed, you can say to this mulberry tree, 'Be pulled up by the roots and be planted in the sea,' and it would obey you.* (Luke 17:5-6). Yet nobody has ever done it! In these days of technology, He would perhaps use a different image to illustrate his point and say, "If you have faith as a thin fuse wire, the full mains voltage of God can come to you." By the way, unbelief blows the fuse, not God's voltage.

> *If you have faith as a thin fuse wire, the full mains voltage of God can come to you.*

## Here are five facts about faith:

1. Faith is your spiritual hand simply accepting what is offered.

2. Faith is not a possession. It is decision, action, believing.

3. Faith is greatest when you are least aware of it, when you act like a trusting child.

4. Faith is letting God pick you up and carry you like a trusting child.

5. Faith is leaving things to God.

If you feel that you lack faith, do not worry, you can get faith for *faith comes by hearing, and hearing by the word of God* (Romans 10:17). The 'why' part brings you the Word of God. Read it again and again, then go and hear it preached. Check your 'fuse'! Cast your doubts away, repent of unbelief, change your mind, and ask for the laying-on of hands.

# THE BONUS

One final word: if you want healing only, you will miss a lot. Healing was made possible by the Cross, but Christ died to do much more than doctors. He died to bring us the far greater blessing of salvation, the forgiveness of sins and peace with God. He is not only a Healer, but a Savior. Jesus said it was better to enter into life maimed than into hell fire whole (Matthew 18:8; Mark 9:43).

To accept healing but reject Christ is disastrous. In fact, millions of people are never healed because they reject the Healer. He does not send healing. He brings it Himself. It is better to be saved than healed. Even better still is to have both: to receive Christ Himself, the Savior and Healer. *How shall He not with Him also freely give us all things?* (Romans 8:32)

☙

# How to Receive a

# MIRACLE FROM GOD

# HOW TO RECEIVE A MIRACLE FROM GOD

## MIRACLE TERRITORY

New Testament believers did not go around searching and probing 'to get a miracle.' They lived on miracle territory. They were in the kingdom of God, and they perceived the miracle-working hand of God in every situation. Believers understood everyday-Christianity to be miraculous, miracles through and through. That theme is common in the letters of the apostle Paul.

Regrettably, what was normal then is not normal now. So much emphasis has been placed upon finding new methods for miracles that it sounds as if it were all a profound secret. We need to remove the mystery and get back to the *simplicity that is in Christ* (2 Corinthians 11:3). Therefore, we shall look at a miracle and then see something greater.

## THE TEACHING COURSE BEGINS

We begin with a lesson by Christ Himself.

> *Now in the fourth watch of the night Jesus went to them, walking on the sea. And when the disciples saw Him walking on the sea, they were troubled, saying, "It is a ghost!" And they cried out for fear.*
>
> *But immediately Jesus spoke to them, saying, "Be of good cheer! It is I; do not be afraid."*
>
> *And Peter answered Him and said, "Lord, if it is You, command me to come to You on the water."*

*So He said, "Come." And when Peter had come down out of the boat, he walked on the water to go to Jesus.* (Matthew 14:25-29)

As we study this, we shall discover three basic elements, or dynamics, of miracles, but first, let us look carefully at the background.

## WHERE THE MIRACLE BEGAN

As the disciples crossed the Sea of Galilee at dawn, they saw a human form gliding across the water, silhouetted against the eastern sky. They rubbed their eyes. Was it a hallucination? But it did not go away. It was real, something neither they, nor anyone else, had ever seen. They broke out in a cold sweat and cried out hoarse with terror.

Two minutes later, there was further consternation among them. Peter jumped over the side of the boat. What is more, he did not plunge into the water as they had expected, but landed on it as if it were an asphalt road! His feet hit the water with a bump, not a splash. Now there were two figures walking the waves!

## TWO IMPORTANT FACTS

First. Miracle conditions began while Peter was still in the boat. Suddenly, he became different. One minute panicking, his hair standing on end, and the next minute daring to do what no mere man had ever done – walk on water.

When Peter changed, the situation changed. Peter found things different when he was different. Some people accept things as they are, and then blame what they are on where they are. However, we know that when Christ comes into someone's life, then heaven works things out. Situations can be changed. That is a great biblical truth.

If we look more carefully at the story of Peter, we shall see something even greater than Peter's circumstances changing. Nothing had changed in Peter's environment. The water looked exactly the same. But Peter had changed; he had become master of the circumstances. The sea billows still rolled, but Peter walked over them; he made a doormat of them. Jesus saves us, our households, and the things around us (Acts 16:31). Miracles begin within us and then affect our surroundings. The sea threatened Peter, opening its foaming mouth to swallow him, but Peter made it an open thoroughfare when Jesus called him to come.

*Situations can be changed. That is a great biblical truth.*

Second. It was Christ Himself who put the disciples where they were; He *made his disciples get into the boat and go before him to the other side* (Matthew 14:22). Yet the boat was *tossed by the waves, for the wind was contrary* (Matthew 14:24). So troubles may arise when we are, or even because we are, doing God's explicit will, but we must give God time, and let Him work things together for good (Romans 8:28). Jesus, in fact, was in charge; He had seen them struggling out on the Sea of Galilee when He was up on the hillside (Mark 6:47-48). Do not worry, the Lord has good eyesight.

God does not guarantee us everlastingly calm seas and prosperous voyages. Even Paul was shipwrecked three times. The disciples were fighting the elements in one of the lumbering boats of their day for the very reason that that was where God wanted them.

Many people feel disillusioned about this very thing. They do what is right and suffer for it. But we need not worry. The trouble, which comes when God puts us where He wants us, is a miracle in the making. The stormy winds of Galilee were the first component for a wonder for Peter and his companions.

We cannot say that all our troubles are in that category. Difficulties do not always indicate that we are doing God's will. Sometimes, they show that we are doing our own will. We land ourselves with problems. For that matter, *man is born to trouble, as the sparks fly upward* as Eliphaz said to Job (Job 5:7); it is 'natural' in our fallen world. Also there is a devil.

Whether a situation is our fault or not, we all need a miracle sometime or other. Difficulties arise for all of us at times, perhaps in health, occupation, marriage, family, or some other area of our lives. Some people find their sins and failures rattling around behind them, the skeletons getting out of the cupboard! Like the disciples in their boat, we can sit amid waves of worry, conjuring up haunting specters – even Jesus was part of the disciples' fears. They needed a miracle, nothing less would do.

> *God does not guarantee us everlastingly calm seas and prosperous voyages.*

Thank God, that He did not intend us to live our lives without miracles. His original plan was that, even after we had done our best, we would still be dependent upon Him to meet our needs. Now we come to the three dynamics of a miracle.

# DYNAMIC #1

## WALKING ON THE WORD

Peter suddenly threw off fears like a suit of old clothes. His change in attitude left his friends at the oars gasping in astonishment. This was no mere impulse; it was propulsion. How?

It began with a voice. The voice of the One who is the Word. That voice rang across the lake. It was Jesus, the voice that raised the very dead (Mark 5:22-24, 35-43; Luke 7:11-15, 8:41-56; John 11:1-44).

It was the most wonderful sound ever to fall on human ears. He himself was the Word (John 1:1).

This Jesus is the living Word. Referring to the Word many years later, Peter said *you do well to heed as a light that shines in a dark place* (2 Peter 1:19). It transforms men and women (Romans 8:2), strengthening their feeble hands, steadying knees that give way (Isaiah 35:3; Hebrews 12:12), and putting new heart into the disheartened.

> *If we wish to hear the living Word, then we must turn to the written Word.*

If we wish to hear the living Word, then we must turn to the written Word. People ignore Scripture, and merely pick up the latest book to learn some new technique. The Word of God is the first secret. Peter knew Christ's voice, but many people seeking miracles do not know the Word of God.

# DYNAMIC #2

## WALKING BY FAITH

Jesus called Peter. His words could have calmed the sea, but instead they calmed Peter, or rather stirred him up. *Be of good cheer! It is I; do not be afraid* (Matthew 14:27). Literally, 'I AM (Greek *ego eimi*). Do not have phobia.' Peter looked across the white tops of the waves, and at first Jesus was part of his fear. Then Jesus said, "*It is I.*" His assurance was carried on the winds. He was Master of it all, and He said, "*It is I.*"

Peter heard Jesus. For that matter, so did the other disciples, but they continued to sit in the boat, and did not climb overboard like Peter. Were they waiting for Jesus to do something, since He had put them there? Perhaps they thought, "He told us to take this trip, so we must bow to His will."

So often people take that position. They think that the Lord has called them to suffer, to endure some misery, and they have no intention of trying to alter what they conceive to be the will of God. They cite Paul's thorn in the flesh – but Paul sought to have God remove it three times (2 Corinthians 12:7-8).

> *Jesus showed us that we can defeat the storm, defeat the devil, overcome evil, and change the world.*

Well, neither Peter nor Jesus took that attitude. Peter knew that Jesus could and would change things. Some people may bow passively to Fate, or Kismet, resigned to unalterable Destiny, accepting whatever comes as if heaven had decreed it. That is not the Christian faith. Faith defies Fate! Jesus showed us that we can defeat the storm, defeat the devil, overcome evil, and change the world. God Himself never changes (Malachi 3:6), but He changes the scenery on the stage of life.

## PETER CHALLENGED JESUS TO CHALLENGE HIM

Peter knew Jesus. He asked this figure that was walking on the sea saying, "It is I," for proof of His identity. He was not going to believe any spirit, or any supernatural experience. *Test the spirits, whether they are of God* (1 John 4:1). The devil can operate supernaturally. Jesus had given warnings that Satan wants *to deceive, if possible, even the elect* (Matthew 24:24). The powers of witches, witch doctors, occultists, and others are not in doubt.

But how do we know they are counterfeit? The hallmark of Calvary love is missing. They all fail to deliver anybody from the guilt and power of sin (John 8:36; Romans 8:2). At best they bring a false sense of peace and final terrible disenchantment.

Now, one unique characteristic of Christ was that He commanded the impossible, and made it possible. Peter therefore applied the test. Peter knew that Jesus would only have to order something, and then he, Peter, could do it. He did not shout, "Lord, if it is you, still the storm." Peter made his query personal: *"Lord, if it is You, command me to come to You on the water"* (Matthew 14:28).

He knew that Jesus did not always caress His disciples and cuddle them for comfort, like a mother her children. He had a disturbing way of throwing out challenges to people to rise above themselves. Peter touched the very heart of Christ by challenging Jesus to challenge him. Any presentation of Christ that does not show Him like that is not worth very much; it is a poor picture of Him. Our message is: repent, forsake your sin, believe, and be saved – the miracle of salvation. Because Christ commands us, it can and will happen.

> *Christ commanded the impossible, and made it possible.*

There is a startling twist to our Bible story. It says that the Lord *would have passed them by* (Mark 6:48)! He showed no inclination to still the storm. This was one of those occasions when Jesus had better plans. The Lord wanted to teach His disciples a lesson of active trust, not apathetic submission. He would have walked past them to the shore while they still strained at the oars of their sodden craft, and there would have been no miracle. Did they want it that way? Was that the size of their faith? Jesus was approaching. He knew where they were; He had put them there, and He had a purpose in keeping them there. Would they react properly? Well, one man did.

## CHANCE OF A MIRACLE

If Jesus, the Lord of miracles, was around, walking miraculously on the water, then Peter was not about to miss the chance. Other miracles could happen. Why let him pass by? Peter certainly did not.

Unfortunately, people do let the Lord of miracles pass by. If there is a Jesus, why live as if there were not? If there is a Father in heaven, why live like orphans? If there is a Savior, why die unsaved? If there is a Healer, why not ask Him to heal? If there is an all-sufficient Christ, why scratch and scrape like chickens in a farmyard?

If things can go wrong, they can also go right. If the devil can work, so can God. How many people expect it? Faith is for the day of calamity, but that is when some believers stop believing. Their faith only flourishes in glorious meetings. They wear their life jackets on deck, but throw them away when they fall into the sea.

> *If things can go wrong, they can also go right.*

So Peter went in for a miracle. Why not, if God is a God of miracles? Live by faith! That is life as God meant it to be. Miracles come to those who live the way of faith. That is God's grand design for our lives, for us to step out, depending on the Word of God and the power of God to give us miracles. We cannot walk with God without experiencing wonders.

## WHAT IS A MIRACLE?

What is a miracle – just a rare event of such great magnitude that it silences critics? Many people do not recognize a miracle when they see one. Christ fed the multitude out of a boy's lunch-basket, and then the wise and learned demanded that He show them a miracle (John 6:1-13, 25-30)! Jesus said that people would not believe, even if someone were to rise from the dead (Luke 16:31). The carnal mind is too dulled to receive the things of God but sharp enough to rationalize all the works of God.

"Miracle" in Scripture is a simple word meaning 'a work of power' – just that. It is not the absurd magic of Roman myth, which our word miracle really signifies. Miracles are things that all believers should experience constantly, the power of God at work in our lives 365-miracle-packed days every year, 366 in a leap year.

> *Miracles are things that all believers should experience constantly.*

We do not appreciate how divine some events are. God conceals His hand. He does not sound a trumpet before Him when He makes the grass grow, or when He works for us. Too often we hear Christians relating what the devil has done, as if the devil were a lot more active than the Lord. Maybe Satan's style is more showy to impress us, but God goes to the heart of the matter, which is to satisfy His heart of love.

## MIRACLE WATERS

When Peter saw Jesus, he saw a miracle happening. Where He was on the lake – that was the place, miracle waters. As long as Peter sat in the boat, there was no miracle. Peter decided to get into that other area so that there would be a miracle. Peter was not going to pass up this miracle chance.

*The just shall live by faith* (Romans 1:17). There is a life where trust in God brings His daily wonders. We can cling to our little boats of doubt, and struggle against the elements, or we can step out for God. He will not let us down.

Peter called to Jesus, *"Lord, if it is You, command me to come to You on the water"* (Matthew 14:28). Why should Jesus agree to such a proposal? Why, because that is Jesus. When you cast yourself on Him, it is for a life of wonders. It does not mean that we can stroll across Lake Erie whenever we fancy, instead of taking the ferry, or walk on the ocean out of bravado, or pick up snakes (Mark 16:18) just to put God to the test (Matthew 4:7; Luke 4:12). That kind of presumption is as heathen as fire walking. Jesus would not make bread from stones simply to prove that He could (Matthew 4:1-4; Luke 4:1-4), but He multiplied the loaves, when empty stomachs needed it (Matthew 14:13-21, 15:32; Mark 6:30-44, 8:1-9; Luke 9:10-17). The kingdom of God is open to us. Too many people step over its border with only one nervous foot. Peter went with both feet at once.

> *When Peter saw Jesus, he saw a miracle happening.*

## THE ENABLING COMMAND

Jesus said just one word: "Come!" There we have it, the first essential for a miracle: the Word of God. In a way it is true that Peter walked on the water, but from the divine angle he was seen to be walking on the Word of God. He put one foot on 'C,' the next on 'O,' stepped onto the 'M' and then onto the 'E.' It worked! The Word of God made all things, and Peter found the water as stable and solid as dry land. There he was walking up the bigger waves and stepping over the little ones without getting even the soles of his sandals damp. He was possibly drier out of the boat than in it.

*"For nothing is impossible with God,"* said the angel Gabriel to Mary (Luke 1:37). Jesus said, *"All things are possible to him who believes"* (Mark 9:23). The Word of God is safe to believe, and safe to walk on. Jesus wants to graft that truth into our very characters. He wants to

make it second nature for us to believe the Word, and to step out on the Word. We can do what we would otherwise never attempt, and live lives that demonstrate the Word at every step. If we doubt the Word, we will fail; but when He appears and speaks, fears melt like snow in the sun.

## MIRACLE ENVIRONMENT

Those who receive the message of the Gospel are in God's miracle environment gladly. I can safely say that ninety-eight percent of a divine miracle is the power of the Word of God. God speaks, and that is His way of doing things; He said, *"Let there be light," and there was light* (Genesis 1:3).

Jesus spoke, and demons fled by the legion (Mark 5:1-20), cemeteries were shaken, lepers were cleansed (Matthew 8:2-4; Mark 1:40-44; Luke 5:12-14, 17:11-14), storms were stilled (Matthew 8:18, 23-27; Mark 4:35-41; Luke 8:22-25), and multitudes were fed (Matthew 14:13-21, 15:32; Mark 6:30-44, 8:1-9; Luke 9:10-17). His words disarmed the temple police trying to arrest Him. They said, "No man ever spoke like this Man" (John 7:46). He spoke with authority. Let people listen to the preaching of the Word. That is the power pack – the Gospel.

> *The Word of God is safe to believe, and safe to walk on.*

When I first saw the significance of the word COME spoken by Jesus, I said, "Lord, if I had such a personal word from you as Peter did, I would jump too. But I am living two thousand years later." At that moment, the Holy Spirit whispered in my heart, "Read Matthew 11:28!" I did, and there it was: *"*COME *to Me,* ALL *you who labor and are heavy laden, and I will give you rest."*

COME to Me, ALL you! This means everyone, including you and me – no one is excluded. Because Jesus Christ has not changed, nor has the power of His Word, miracles will happen today for all of us. The number one dynamic, the Word of God, actually produces number two, the dynamic of faith. *Faith comes by hearing, and hearing by the word of God* (Romans 10:17).

## THE WORD IMPARTS THE POWER
## TO BELIEVE IN THE WORD

The words of Jesus cause us to trust. They generate their own authority, and carry their own built-in convictions. We can choose to trust them, or not to trust them. We can resist them. That is a matter of choice. Anybody can choose not to believe. Doubt is not a sign of brilliance. Anybody can choose to believe. Faith is a decision; it is a matter of attitude. The Word breathes life into lifeless souls – if they want to live. There is the invitation, COME, and we can come, striding across the sea if need be, when He bids us.

> *The number one dynamic, the Word of God, actually produces number two, the dynamic of faith.*

Peter heard and believed. If he had not, would there have been a miracle? The answer is a resounding no! In fact, the miracle stopped when Peter stopped believing. *But when he saw that the wind was boisterous, he was afraid; and beginning to sink he cried out, saying, "Lord, save me!"* (Matthew 14:30). Of course, Jesus did save him, but that was an anticlimax after such a bold venture of faith.

Having faith is necessary to experience signs and wonders (Mark 16:17-18; Hebrews 11:6). It is a vital part of the miracle circuit. It is faith in Christ Jesus, not just faith in the power of faith, but faith in the power of God. Not faith in ourselves, that we can do this or that, or that something marvelous will happen, but faith in God. Faith is not in miracles, but in Jesus, who makes them happen – and faith means still believing, even when He does not make them happen. He supervises the whole operation, because He is the One who initiated it and involved us by calling us.

> *Faith in Christ Jesus is faith in the power of God.*

This story, somewhat like a parable, has remained with me since my Sunday School days. As a farmer walked across his field, he heard a mouse squeaking. He looked, and a small drama unfolded before his eyes. A snake had hypnotized a mouse. It was paralyzed. All the rodent could do was squeak. The snake edged closer and closer. Then, the story goes, the farmer took out his big handkerchief, and put it between the snake and the mouse. The spell was broken; the mouse could move, and it darted away, free.

This might only be a children's story, but of one thing I am certain, many people are paralyzed by a spirit of fear. It is the hypnotic power of that serpent of old, who is the devil and Satan (Revelation 20:2). People brood over sickness and death. We listen to medical experts, and begin to tremble and mourn. Fear reduces us to inaction, and it prostrates us. The jaws of grief open to devour us.

Then comes the Word of God – God's big 'pocket handkerchief' is let down between us and that hypnotizing, paralyzing, and obsessing terror. The Word of God creates new trust and hope. If we let it! *Therefore if the Son makes you free, you shall be free indeed* (John 8:36).

We may have faith in doctors or other medical experts. They speak within the province of their particular knowledge; they offer only medical opinions, and those can sometimes vary. We can get a second opinion: the Word of God. It is common for medical facts to be interpreted in isolation, out of context to a patient's circumstances. That is not scientific in the truest sense. All facts must be taken into account, and one of those facts is a patient's faith in what the Word of God says.

Faith is believing God more than we believe our feelings, more than our apprehensions. True faith is always in someone – in Jesus, in what He said, is saying, and in what He is doing. People create such difficulties about believing God. Does a child have any difficulty trusting an adult when lifted into his or her arms? Does a four-year-old say, "I don't know whether I have enough faith to let you pick me up"? Children do not have such thoughts, only adults! A child knows nothing about faith, yet exercises it. The more faith we have, the less we notice it. Faith, in the end, is nothing at all; it is just letting God do what He says He will do. In fact, the first dynamic of a miracle, the Word of God, is ninety-eight percent of it, and faith is only one percent. Faith is only the hand by which we take what God offers. That is all that is needed.

> *Faith is believing God more than we believe our feelings.*

The miracle-power circuit is almost closed, but there is one more thing – the remaining one percent.

# DYNAMIC #3

## ACTING IN OBEDIENCE

So, Peter heard the word of Jesus, and believed it. But no miracle occurred. Something was missing. What was the missing link? The last secret is obedience, or action. Peter had to jump overboard. He went overboard for God. He leaped into a miracle.

This explains a lot. It points out a problem that is quite common. Why is it that so many good Christians never personally experience the miracle-working power of God in their lives? They sit so faithfully in their seats at church, listening to the best preachers, even weeping, praying, and confessing, "Lord, I believe." They hear the Word and believe it. Then what? They do not go overboard for God. They just sit there, waiting for Jesus to do something, praying, "Lord, send the power," and He passes by their boats.

If we want things to happen, we must get out of our boats, and move in line with Jesus, walking the waves. He is calling us. He does not say, "Hold tight. I'll soon be with you in the boat." He says, "Come." What, on the water? Yes! That is where the miracles happen.

> *If we want things to happen, we must get out of our boats, and move in line with Jesus, walking the waves.*

The boat may be just a symbol of our own little ideas. We make them up ourselves. We collect them to form 'bits of' creeds, made up of bits of books, bits of sermons, and bits of stories, like birds collecting straw and string to make their nests: "The days of miracles are passed"; "It is God's will for me to be sick because He has something for me to learn." Here is that nest, or that boat. People row these comfortable little boats contentedly for years, believing that eventually they will reach port. They are satisfied to listen to testimonies, or to witness the miracle-working power of God in the lives of others, but if they would go overboard for God, they could walk on the miracle waters themselves.

When Peter went overboard, he rocked the boat. To see God in action, we must be in action ourselves, whether we rock the boat or not. Do not worry about the doubters, whom we may disturb. If we are comfortably settled in unchallenging company, where there is no real obedience of faith, then we must jump over the side, right over human opinion, and make for Jesus out there in the miracle waters.

Jump! We *shall not die, but live, and declare the works of the Lord* (Psalm 118:17). The religious thinker and writer, Kierkegaard, spoke of faith as a leap into the dark, but it is not. It is a leap out of the dark into the light. The blind man leapt out of his darkness into the pool of Siloam, and light broke upon his vision (John 9). The waters will not swallow us, but will carry us, like the waters of the flood, which bore believing Noah, while drowning the whole world of scoffers.

The whitecaps that snarled and roared, dashing Peter's boat, suddenly became horses to carry him on his way to Jesus. Destroy us? Jesus destroyed destruction at the cross. He will not come and carry us piggyback. He smiles, beckons, and says, "Come."

Obedience puts the plug in, and the power begins to work. It is the final connection. Remember what Smith Wigglesworth told a conventional doubting clergyman: "The Acts of the Apostles was written because the apostles acted."

# LET US WRITE A FEW MORE CHAPTERS OURSELVES

༄

# THE GIFT of REDEMPTION

# FOREWORD

What are the two greatest things God ever did? The Bible tells us that He created the heavens and the earth. Could anything possibly equal that – making our wonderful world, with its oceans, mountains and rivers, and filling the heavens with stars?

In fact, God did do something else that was far more difficult. We call it the work of Redemption. Creation cost God nothing, but that next task cost him everything.

At creation God blessed us with the energies of life. Then He blessed us with the gift of Redemption, adding new life to ordinary life. Millions of people around the world enjoy it. They are jubilant. They exclaim and sing: "I am redeemed!" They cannot keep quiet about this wonderful gift that God has given them.

Unfortunately, not everyone is alive in this way, because not everyone is redeemed. And sadly, some people have never even heard of Redemption. Redemption is like creation – nobody thought of it but God. It never crossed anyone's mind, not even that of the wisest person who ever lived. There are many religions in the world, but none of them offers Redemption. People believe in many different gods, but not one of them is a redeemer. There are many holy books, but only one of them brings us the good news of Redemption – the Bible.

As you read this – and as you read the Bible for yourself – our prayer is that you will come to know God's Redemption for yourself. May God bless you with all the good things He longs to give you!

# THE GIFT OF REDEMPTION

## WHAT IS REDEMPTION?

The word 'Redemption' comes from 'redeem,' which means 'to buy back something which once belonged to you.' One dictionary definition puts it like this:

- Redemption: To recover possession or ownership by payment of a price. Deliverance from sin through the incarnation, sufferings, and death of Christ.

- To redeem something also means to obtain it by paying ransom.

The Bible explains Redemption by using pictures or models. The greatest of its pictures is the story of how God freed the people of Israel from their slavery in Egypt. From that time on, God was known as the Redeemer. This tremendous event changed the world, but it was still only a small sketch of the great Redemption to come.

Alongside this great event, there are several other biblical pictures. As we look at them, they will help us to appreciate how marvelous Redemption is.

## THE ISRAELITES IN EGYPT

Israel is the only nation in history that was redeemed. This was something that was achieved by God – the people of Israel did not do it themselves.

Note: Throughout this chapter, 'Redemption' appears with a capital letter 'R' to signify eternal Redemption.

The Israelites were trapped in Egypt, and were cruelly subjected to forced labor by the Egyptians. After many years of this slavery, the Lord said:

> *I am the LORD; I will bring you out from under the burdens of the Egyptians, I will rescue you from their bondage, and I will redeem you with an outstretched arm and with great judgments. I will take you as My people, and I will be your God.* (Exodus 6:6-7)

And this was exactly what He did. He sent His servant Moses to the King of Egypt, with the famous instruction: *Let my people go.* At first the King resisted God and refused to release the people of Israel. But eventually, after God had sent ten plagues upon the land of Egypt, the Israelites were able to escape – through the power and love of God.

This amazing event is called 'The Exodus.' Today we might call it 'The Great Escape.' You can read the full story in the first few chapters of the book of Exodus. The Exodus also tells us three very important things about Redemption.

1. GOD ACTED FREELY. God stepped into this desperate situation, acting entirely on His own initiative. He did not rescue His people because He had to, or because He was bound by duty. He did it freely; reclaiming what rightfully belonged to Him.

2. GOD ACTED FOR HIS PEOPLE. The dictionary definition makes it clear that you can only redeem what you have once owned. God said that the people of Israel were His people. They belonged to Him.

3. GOD ACTED OUT OF LOVE. God redeemed the people of Israel because of His great love for them. What He did shows what He really is at heart. Just as someone might be a musician or an artist by gift and nature, so God is a loving Redeemer. As one of the Bible's

prophets said: *"All flesh shall know that I, the LORD, am your Savior, and your Redeemer, the Mighty One of Jacob"* (Isaiah 49:26).

## REDEMPTION IS FOR ALL MANKIND

The wonderful story of the Exodus might make us think that Redemption was just for one particular nation at one particular time in the past. But that is not true. Redemption is much bigger than that.

The truth is that all mankind needs Redemption. Redemption did not occur just once for one small race. That was like a mere demonstration! The Exodus story tells us about God, and it shows us what He is like – not just what He *was like* then, but what He *is always like*, and for everybody. This is because God never changes, and as we will see, He provided Redemption on a world scale and for all eternity.

The great problem on earth has always been sin. Just as the people of Israel were in slavery to their Egyptian masters, so human beings are in slavery to sin. Nobody but God Himself could possibly break its grip.

*To redeem all mankind from sin, God sent His own Son from heaven.*

To release Israel from Egypt, God simply hurled plagues down from the heavens. But to redeem all mankind from sin, He sent His own Son from heaven. Jesus Christ is the only one who could ever truly claim to be the Redeemer. Only He could ever take on the task of Redemption. He is the Holy One, the sinless Son of God, Jesus Christ the Lord.

## SEVEN FACTS ABOUT REDEMPTION

1. It is not just an idea or a subject to learn – it is something that happens to you.

2. It is not just an experience you once had – it goes on throughout your life.

3. It is not just a feeling – it is a new direction and purpose in life.

4. It is not just being good and sincere – it is becoming a new person.

5. It is not 'religion', or something that you do – it is what God does.

6. It is not a human invention – it is God's business.

7. It is no credit to us – Redemption brings praise to God for eternity.

## WHY DOES GOD REDEEM?

If nobody needed Redemption, God would not have sent Christ to redeem us. The French philosopher Jean-Jacques Rousseau said, "Man was born free but everywhere is in chains." The Bible puts it like this: "*The whole world lies under the sway of the wicked one*" (1 John 5:19).

The devil, described in the Bible as *the prince of the power of the air, the spirit who now works in the sons of disobedience* (Ephesians 2:2), has seduced everybody. There are a million temptations, urges, habits, and addictions. They drive people like the whips of the Egyptian taskmasters.

But then we read that Christ came and *went about doing good and healing all who were oppressed by the devil, for God was with Him* (Acts 10:38).

If we come to God, we must know what He is like and what to expect of Him. If we go to the doctor, it is for medicine. If we go to a counselor, it is for good advice. So when we come to God, we come to Him as Redeemer.

> *To know God we must first come to Him as our Savior and our Redeemer.*

What does this mean? God is a Redeemer, and so we must meet Him first for Redemption. Some treat Him as the Almighty, or as the King, or for answers to prayer, without really knowing Him. He is often gracious to them. He is, of course, the Almighty and the King of all kings, but to know Him we must first come to Him as our Savior and our Redeemer. The first thing He wants is to save us, redeem us, and restore us to our true owner – our Maker and Father.

When this happens, we are set free. Jesus said: *"If the Son makes you free, you shall be free indeed"* (John 8:36).

There are two reasons why God redeems us. First, He owns us. Second, we turned away from God and were lost to Him. Let us look at these two reasons in turn.

## WE ALL BELONG TO GOD

We saw earlier that you cannot redeem what you never owned. We can see this clearly in the picture of God redeeming Israel. God was their rightful owner.

On one occasion God says: *"This people I have formed for Myself"* (Isaiah 43:21) – and here He is talking not just about the individuals,

but about the whole nation. He formed the nation Himself –
providing it with His laws, His leaders, and His land. "They are
My servants," He said, *"whom I brought out* [or redeemed] *of Egypt"*
(Leviticus 25:55).

Not only Israel but every person ever born once belonged to God.
The Creator owns what He creates. We have children for ourselves
and so does God. The Bible expresses it in this way:

> *The earth is the Lord's, and everything in it, the world,
> and all who live in it.* (Psalm 24:1)

> *Know that the Lord is God. It is He who made us, and
> we are His; we are His people, the sheep of His pasture.*
> (Psalm 100:3)

The Bible also says about God: *You created all things, and by Your will
they exist and were created* (Revelation 4:11). All of us belong to God
– and so all of us can be redeemed by Him.

## A FORFEITED POSSESSION

Let us look at Israel again. They belonged to God, but they also
sinned against Him. The story of the Exodus tells us that they bowed
down and served the Egyptian gods. Even though they did this, it
did not alter the fact that God had been the God of their ancestors
– and that He was still their God.

He remembered the promises He had made to the people of Israel,
and this is why He told Moses: *"I have come down to deliver them out
of the hand of the Egyptians"* (Exodus 3:8).

Even after that history-making deliverance of the Exodus, the people
forgot God, but He did not forget them. In a famous passage,
God says:

*I reared children and brought them up, but they have rebelled against Me. The ox knows his master, the donkey his owner's manger, but Israel does not know.* (Isaiah 1:2-3)

There were times when God seemed to be on the verge of completely rejecting His people: Then God said: *"You are not My people, and I will not be your God"* (Hosea 1:9). But He was still their rightful Lord, and His love for them would not let them go. Therefore, He said, *"How can I give you up?"* (Hosea 11:8).

Because they belonged to God, He delivered them time after time, from disaster after disaster. He said, *"You shall know that I, the LORD, am your Savior and your Redeemer, the Mighty One of Jacob"* (Isaiah 60:16).

## ADDICTED TO SIN

The world today desperately needs the Redemption of God that does not give us up. All around us we can see how people turn away from God, even though they desperately need His love.

Money, military might, evil desires and selfishness are tyrannies, which seem to rule everything. Many people are also driven by superstition and fear. In Africa, people who become Christians bring their witchcraft items and symbols to be burnt publicly.

But it is not only in Africa that ungodly things rule people's lives. Millions throughout the world are ruled by the stars and spirits, or dominated by drugs and other addictions. While the men and women of the sports arena or the silver screen are idolized, God is forgotten. The Bible is speaking about us, and the things we worship, when it says: *Here are your gods* (1 Kings 12:28).

Millions hide from God as if He were their worst enemy. This is how it has been from the very beginning. God had to go searching in the Garden of Eden for Adam and Eve, calling: *"Adam, where are you?"* (Genesis 3:9). The Bible says that *we all, like sheep, have gone astray, each of us has turned to his own way* (Isaiah 53:6).

Paul, in the New Testament, calls people *the sons of disobedience* (Ephesians 2:2), who are in *the snare of the devil, having been taken captive by him to do his will* (2 Timothy 2:26). Nothing has changed.

And he also says:

> *Do you not know that to whom you present yourselves slaves to obey, you are that one's slaves whom you obey, whether of sin leading to death, or of obedience leading to righteousness?* (Romans 6:16)

Nobody can deny those Scriptures.

The Bible's picture of our world is of the strong man Samson, who loved Delilah and fell asleep with his head on her lap while she treacherously plotted his destruction. The world is comfortable in the lap of the devil, *having been taken captive by him to do his will* (2 Timothy 2:26).

*Each of us knows the bitterness of failure. Sin affects the way the whole world is run.*

Each of us knows the bitterness of failure. Sin affects the way the whole world is run. It destroys nations, just as it destroyed Israel. Every news program proves it. Only bad news is news. If we started a list of our common evils we would never finish it.

The Bible tells us about the terrible effects of all this: *Your iniquities have separated you from your God* (Isaiah 59:2). And it also asks one of the biggest questions that we can ever ask: *"How then can a man be righteous before God? How can one born of woman be pure?"* (Job 25:4)

## HELP FROM OUTSIDE OURSELVES

The only answer in the world to this question is in the Bible. It is an answer that goes right to the heart of Redemption.

This is why Redemption is not about 'going religious' – it is not as trivial as that. Instead, Redemption is as much a part of things as creation. The whole of human existence is poisoned by evil, but God has given us the antidote: Redemption by Jesus Christ. God never sold us out to the devil. He has ownership rights and responsibilities. He sent Jesus to begin the work of Redemption, and He will complete it.

Nobody can redeem themselves. Of course, some people think they can. They talk about living good, honest lives – but they still give God the cold shoulder. And when you think about it, a good honest slave is still a slave! He or she needs someone to set them free.

Or think of it in this way. We all blot our copybooks. If we turn over a new leaf, the old blotted leaves are still there. We need help to wipe away those blots, help that we cannot give ourselves. To redeem us cost Jesus the most awful effort – with grief, sweat, blood, tears, and the agony of a public execution. If Jesus had to go through all this, how could you or I possibly redeem ourselves?

For thousands of years the heart of the human dilemma has been sin. We cannot free ourselves. We cannot make forgiveness for ourselves. And this is because sin goes right to the heart of us. The human heart, the Bible says, *is deceitful above all things, and desperately wicked* (Jeremiah 17:9).

No surgeon can operate and give us a sinless heart. No therapist can rid us of selfishness or hate. Science can do wonders, but science itself needs saving because it brings great evils as well as good. No computer could number our sins, or come up with a solution. The saints and the best people who ever lived shed hopeless tears over the evils of their own heart. But in the face of all this bad news, there is good news – Jesus saves!

> *No surgeon can operate and give us a sinless heart.*

## SOMEONE WHO WAS "GOOD ENOUGH"

Think back for a moment to the story of the Exodus. After four hundred years in Egypt, nobody was able to redeem the Israelites from their slavery. Moses was the greatest leader they ever had, but even he was not perfect. Later in the story, when Israel sinned and God spoke of blotting them all out, Moses offered his own life to ransom the nation. It was bluntly refused. Moses was simply not good enough to achieve redemption for his people.

There never was anyone good enough to stand before God and deliver the world. In the words of a famous Christian hymn: "There was no other good enough to pay the price of sin." The Bible is right when it says: *"There is none righteous, no, not one"* (Romans 3:10); *"But we are all like an unclean thing, and all our righteousnesses are like filthy rags"* (Isaiah 64:6).

No man or woman ever wore the jeweled crown of perfection – until the birth of a baby one night in Bethlehem: *But when the fullness of the time had come, God sent forth His Son, born of a woman, born under the law, to redeem those who were under the law, that we might receive the adoption as sons* (Galatians 4:4-5).

The Son of God became the Son of Man. He was the totally unselfish one, living every moment for us. And He was the one who was 'good enough' to pay the price of sin.

## THE ONE AND ONLY REDEEMER

There can never be a joint Redeemer, a co-Savior. It was Jesus Christ who came into the world for us, who suffered and died for us, and who was raised from the dead for us. Neither His foster father Joseph, nor His mother Mary, gave themselves for us. No apostle, no disciple, ever achieved what Jesus achieved for us. God is jealous of His rights as the Redeemer.

Only Jesus could achieve the work of Redemption, because He was not only a human being, but He was God Himself, living on earth. The Bible tells us that God the Father *has delivered us from the power of darkness and conveyed us into the kingdom of the Son of His love, in whom we have redemption through His blood, the forgiveness of sins. He is the image of the invisible God, the firstborn over all creation* (Colossians 1:13-15).

Despite this clear teaching, the false doctrine has been taught that Jesus was nothing but a human being, whom God exalted to sit beside Him. However, no mere creature could ever become God to redeem us. God never became God, or He would not be God, neither could He create another like Himself. No creature can masquerade as the uncreated source of all things. No one can cross that gulf.

It was God – not an angel – who breathed into Adam the breath of life. As the apostle Paul said: *God, who made the world and everything in it ... gives to all life, breath, and all things* (Acts 17:24-25). Only God made us and owns us, and only God can redeem us.

The glorious truth is that while a human being cannot become God, God did become a human being in the person of Jesus Christ, so that He could redeem us. God says:

> *I, even I, am the Lord, and apart from me there is no Savior. I am the Lord; that is my name! I will not give my glory to another. I, the LORD, am your Savior, and your Redeemer.* (Isaiah 43:11, 42:8, 49:26)

This is emphasized in chapter after chapter in the book of Isaiah.

## PAYING THE RANSOM

God redeemed Israel from Egypt, but when we talk about the eternal Redemption of Jesus Christ, there are some big differences.

To begin with, the people of Israel were not redeemed from their sin, but only from Egypt. Because of their sins and faithlessness, they all died in the wilderness, and only their children entered the land God had promised them. Then again, God gave no ransom, and Egypt got nothing for its hostages. God simply took what belonged to Him. It cost Him nothing, and He sent Israel away free. But for eternal Redemption, the payment was infinite.

The words of Jesus Himself give us an important key: *For even the Son of Man did not come to be served, but to serve, and to give His life a ransom for many* (Mark 10:45). This is confirmed by the words of Paul: "*For there is one God and one Mediator between God and men, the Man Christ Jesus, who gave Himself a ransom for all*" (1 Timothy 2:5-6). A ransom is a price paid in exchange for a captive. It is the means of buying his or her freedom.

This does not mean that God paid a ransom into somebody's hands. But He did pay the price. The Son of God was not handed over to

Satan in exchange for his captives. But God *delivered Him up for us all* (Romans 8:32). He surrendered Him into the hands of those who crucified Him. *For God so loved the world that He gave His only begotten Son* (John 3:16).

This was done not for a good world, but for a bad one. *While we were still sinners, Christ died for us* (Romans 5:8). He did not merely visit this world, but gave Himself for us in the most costly way. So that we could belong to Him, He belonged to us. *For Christ also suffered once for sins, the just for the unjust, that He might bring us to God* (1 Peter 3:18).

# THE GREATEST LOVE STORY
# EVER TOLD

The Bible provides us with some moving illustrations of God's love for a lost world. Better than the best romantic novels, they show us His heartache, His utter devotion to us, and His practical solution. And the best thing of all is that it is real – not merely the stuff of fiction.

## THE STORY OF HOSEA

Take, for example, the story of the prophet Hosea's redeeming love. He was a man who was honest and upright, and who was deeply committed to God. Despite this, the Lord told him to marry a wife who was unfaithful. In obedience to God, he did this. Hosea's wife bore children – but he was not their father. He named one of them 'Lo-ammi', which means, 'not my people.'

Despite everything that Hosea did for her, his immoral wife sank lower and lower until she became a slave prostitute in a brothel.

Then God told Hosea to get her back, and more than that, to love her. So Hosea redeemed her, buying back his own wife for a handful of silver – fifteen shekels. He accepted her and loved her again. It was a picture of God's Redemption – a moving story of deep, self-sacrificing love.

The love of God is deeply offended by our sin and unfaithfulness, but the promise God gave to Hosea holds good for the whole world: *I will ransom them from the power of the grave; I will redeem them from death* (Hosea 13:14). We can thank God for that. We see the hell which many people make of their own and other people's lives. Only God can put things right.

Hosea paid fifteen shekels to redeem his wife. But what were we worth to God? Peter, in the New Testament, tells us:

> *Knowing that you were not redeemed with corruptible things, like silver or gold, from your aimless conduct received by tradition from your fathers, but with the precious blood of Christ, as of a lamb without blemish and without spot but with the precious blood of Christ, as of a lamb without blemish and without spot.* (1 Peter 1:18-19)

## THE STORY OF RUTH

Another story from the Bible gives us insight into a second aspect of Redemption – the role of the 'kinsman-redeemer.'

In the Old Testament book of Ruth a man and his wife, Naomi, went with their two sons to live in the land of Moab. They were forced to make this journey, because there was famine in Israel. There the sons married. A few years later, both the sons and their father died, leaving behind three widows.

When Naomi heard that the famine in Israel was over, she decided to return to her homeland. The widow of one son stayed behind in Moab, and went back to her parents. The other, Ruth, clung to her mother-in-law, and loyally refused to leave her. The two women made their way back into Israel, to Bethlehem.

Naomi had land rights there, and so did Ruth, as the widow of an Israeli man. Land in Israel was an inheritance that could never pass into the permanent ownership of another family. It could be leased, but not sold. If the land was forfeited through debt or any other circumstance, the original owner could still claim it back – in other words, he or she could redeem it.

This was all well and good, but Naomi and Ruth had no money to redeem the property. So it had to be done by a relative or kinsman who carried special family responsibilities. In the story of Ruth, a relation came forward called Boaz. But in order to reclaim the estate, Boaz would have to marry her. Now, Boaz had already been impressed by the self-sacrificing character of the young widow, and was willing to assume the full measure of his responsibilities. So, with the full blessing of the leaders of the town, he and Ruth married.

This was how a Moabite – a non-Jewish woman – became the great-grandmother of King David, and an ancestor of Jesus Christ.

## OUR KINSMAN-REDEEMER

The story of Ruth gives us a picture of the great kinsman-redeemer, Jesus Christ. The human family needed a kinsman, a representative, to redeem our lost estate. Someone who was unrelated to us could not do it.

That is why the Bible stresses the humanity of Jesus as well as His divinity:

> *For unto us a Child is born, unto us a Son is given; and the government will be upon His shoulder. Of the increase of His government and peace there will be no end.* (Isaiah 9:6-7)

We can find this in the New Testament, as well: *as the children have partaken of flesh and blood, He Himself likewise shared in the same* (Hebrews 2:14). Jesus, as a member of the human family, was the person God made responsible to redeem mankind's lost rights in the eternal scheme of God.

Actually, Israel certainly never thought of God as a kinsman. To them He seemed an awesome being, the wholly other one, holy and separate. He redeemed them simply by force, snatching them from under the nose of Pharaoh, *with a mighty hand and with an outstretched arm* (Deuteronomy 26:8). Under His feet the Sinai mountain shivered and shook. *The Strength of Israel ... is not a man* (1 Samuel 15:29).

*Jesus secured our eternal inheritance and life with God. Nobody can take away what He paid for on the cross.*

But He who was *not a man* became man, our kinsman. The maker of human beings clothed Himself in the same flesh. How, we do not know – any more than we know how God made heaven and earth. It is a glorious mystery, but *the Word became flesh and dwelt among us* (John 1:14). He whom the heaven of heavens cannot contain became one of us on this planet.

He did more:

> *Being in the form of God, did not consider it robbery to be equal with God, but made Himself of no reputation, taking the form of a bondservant, and coming in the likeness of men. And being found in appearance as a man, He humbled Himself and became obedient to the point of death, even the death of the cross.* (Philippians 2:6-8)

The value of Redemption must be judged by its price. *Christ has redeemed us ... God sent forth His Son ... to redeem those who were under the law* (Galatians 3:13; 4:5). These verses of Paul use a special word for 'redeem' which means 'bought out of.' Christ was our kinsman-redeemer when spiritually, like Ruth and Naomi, we were destitute. He secured our eternal inheritance and life with God. Nobody can take away what Jesus paid for on the cross.

# THE DOWRY

In the East, when a young man saw a girl he wanted to marry, he first had to have his father's permission to seek her hand. Once his father had agreed, the young man went to the girl's home to ask for her father's consent to the marriage.

Next came the matter of the dowry. This was an amount of money, paid perhaps in silver or gold. The amount was settled by negotiation between the two families, and it formally established a legally binding marriage contract.

In this way, the couple became engaged. A year might go by before they married, but they both prepared for it. Then one night, in a torch-lit procession, the young man and his friends went over to the home of the bride, and formally 'kidnapped' her – although she offered no resistance! They were then married, had a honeymoon, and everyone feasted. She was now the young man's 'property.'

These customs are the background to a passage in one of the most famous letters of the New Testament:

> *You were not redeemed with corruptible things, like silver or gold ... but with the precious blood of Christ, as of a lamb without blemish and without spot. He indeed was foreordained before the foundation of the world.* (1 Peter 1:18-20)

# THE ROYAL WEDDING

In the Bible, the company of those who are redeemed are described as *the bride of Christ.* Just as in an Eastern wedding, God the Son came by the Father's will to the house of His bride – this world – to find those who would love Him.

And as in an Eastern wedding, the dowry was the vital issue. The Son paid with His precious blood, His own life.

> *Christ loved the church and gave Himself for her, that He might sanctify and cleanse her with the washing of water by the word, that He might present her to Himself a glorious church, not having spot or wrinkle or any such thing, but that she should be holy and without blemish.* (Ephesians 5:25-27)

No bride ever cost a bridegroom so much: *the church of God, which He purchased with His own blood* (Acts 20:28), and *You are not your own; you were bought at a price* (1 Corinthians 6:19-20).

There was no bargaining. The church was not a cheap bride. Jesus paid the full price. Joseph was sold for twenty silver shekels and Judas sold Christ for thirty pieces of silver, but Christ gave Himself for us. What He did for us made everyone infinitely valuable. Jesus said that a single human soul was worth more than the whole world, and He meant it (Matthew 16:26). He gave all that He had for all that there were.

The payment of the dowry sealed the marriage contract. This is reflected in the Gospel. At the Last Supper, Jesus said, *"This cup is the new covenant in My blood, which is shed for you"* (Luke 22:20). The marriage is arranged: hallelujah! That marriage contract cannot be annulled: *The one who comes to Me I will by no means cast out* (John 6:37).

Soon the Bridegroom will come like an Eastern bridegroom in His torch-lit procession. Everyone will see the coming of the Son of Man, and He will take away His bride. Then the *marriage supper of the Lamb* will take place.

There will be music and joy. Five times in the book of Revelation we read of a new song. The old songs are the Psalms of Israel, but Jesus Christ has changed the worship and we sing, "*You have redeemed us to God by Your blood*" (Revelation 5:9). The people of Israel sang about their redemption from Egypt. Christians sing of their Redemption from sin.

## THE AVENGER

Not all the duties of a kinsman-redeemer were as pleasurable as those related in the story of Ruth and Boaz. In those cruel old days, he also had to be an avenger. If a man was killed, even accidentally, then the kinsman-redeemer had to avenge his death by slaying a man from the killer's family. The blood feud was a merciless, wicked practice, which could go on between families for generations.

God hated this wickedness. In the book of Judges, chapter twenty, He commanded cities of refuge to be appointed for those who were fugitives. A man being pursued by an avenger could flee to a city of refuge. Once he was inside the gates, he was protected.

One example of a kinsman-redeemer avenging a life is found in the second book of Samuel, chapter three. At that time, there was civil war in Israel, and Abner, the king's cousin, killed a man called Asahel. His brother Joab vowed vengeance. He feigned friendship with Abner and invited him to Hebron. They greeted one another outside the gates of the town, but there Joab treacherously stabbed Abner, and he died.

The irony is that Hebron was a city of refuge. A few meters further and Abner would have been inside and safe. It became a saying: *Should Abner die as a fool dies?* (2 Samuel 3:33)

This grim story pictures the danger we are all in. Our sin will find us out. It will haunt us and hunt us even beyond the grave. Judgment is sure, like a pursuing vengeance. The Bible is clear about this: *The soul who sins shall die* (Ezekiel 18:4); *the wages of sin is death* (Romans 6:23).

We need a city of refuge, a Redeemer. We read that God is *longsuffering toward us, not willing that any should perish but that all should come to repentance* (2 Peter 3:9). Our perfect hope is Jesus, because to repent and flee to Him brings us safety.

> *To die and not be in Christ is to die unredeemed, in unbelief, and in our sins.*

The New Testament often talks about being in Christ. Jesus said, "*The one who comes to Me I will by no means cast out*" (John 6:37). If we are not driven away, then we are invited in. Jesus is our city of refuge. As Paul says, "*There is therefore now no condemnation to those who are in Christ Jesus*" (Romans 8:1).

To die and not be in Christ is to die unredeemed, in unbelief, and in our sins. It is to die *as a fool dies* – so near to safety, but foolishly outside the gates of mercy. There is only one place we can go to be saved:

> *The LORD is my rock and my fortress and my deliverer; My God, my strength, in whom I will trust; My shield and the horn of my salvation, my stronghold. I will call upon the LORD, who is worthy to be praised; so shall I be saved from my enemies.* (Psalm 18:2-3)

The greatest tragedy is to be unredeemed, when the Redeemer is so close at hand.

## THE KINSMAN-REDEEMER
## WHO DIED INSTEAD OF KILLING

Our Kinsman-Redeemer, Jesus, did a most wonderful thing. Wicked men had bound Him, lashed, and crucified Him, the innocent one, unlawfully and unjustly. Should His death not be avenged? His followers might have attacked those who were guilty of this atrocity. Peter did strike one blow with his sword when Jesus was arrested, but Jesus told that quick-tempered man to put his sword away.

Jesus did not cry out for vengeance. Instead, as He was being nailed to the cross, He kept on praying: *"Father, forgive them"* (Luke 23:34).

Darkness then shrouded the scene, but from the heart of that blackness shone a bright ray of mercy and reconciliation. Paul expressed it in these words: *God was in Christ reconciling the world to Himself* (2 Corinthians 5:19).

> *For it pleased the Father that in Him all the fullness should dwell, and by Him to reconcile all things to Himself, by Him, whether things on earth or things in heaven, having made peace through the blood of His cross.*
> (Colossians 1:19-20)

Whoever was guilty of Jesus' death, they were forgiven by His prayer, whether they were Greek, Roman, or Jewish. The blood of Jesus that they shed was their Redemption. Their pardon was handed to them at the very cross they erected. It was written by the pen of God dipped in the fountain of the precious blood of Jesus.

For centuries, the so-called 'Christian' nations persecuted the Jewish people as 'Christ killers.' These 'Christians' did not know God, the true account of His death, or the Scriptures. Their religion was corrupt. They were ignorant of its first principle of mercy.

They had no idea about the wonderful spirit of forgiveness of the One they called their Savior and Redeemer. Christ forgave those who slew Him, and who is anybody else to take vengeance?

This was the wonderful thing which Jesus, our Kinsman-Redeemer, did. Instead of coming to avenge our sins, He allowed all the vengeance due to us to fall on Him. He became the great and ultimate victim, blocking the course of the blood feud.

Sin pursued us, demanding the blood of the sinful. But Jesus offered His own blood to put an end to all vengeance.

> For He Himself is our peace, who has made both one, and has broken down the middle wall of separation ... and He came and preached peace to you who were afar off and to those who were near. (Ephesians 2:14, 17)

Peace! Joab slid a keen blade into Abner to take vengeance, but Jesus allowed His own body to receive a spear wound from those who hated Him. He accepted the shame of crucifixion in order to redeem us all. He proclaimed peace and forgiveness, not a 'holy war' against the infidel. He comes to us with pity, not with punishment. His ministry is reconciliation.

*Our Kinsman-Redeemer allowed all the vengeance due to us to fall on Him.*

When people are gripped by the demons of hate and violence, He is *our great God and Savior Jesus Christ, who gave Himself for us, that He might redeem us from every lawless deed and purify for Himself His own special people, zealous for good works* (Titus 2:13-14).

# PRIVILEGE AND RESPONSIBILITY

They say that privilege brings responsibility. Paul once befriended a runaway slave called Onesimus. That young man became a Christian. Paul sent him back to his owner, Philemon, with a letter asking him to forgive Onesimus and take him back. Now the name Onesimus means 'useful,' and Paul made a pun on his name, saying that he, *who once was unprofitable to you, but now, is profitable to you and to me* (Philemon 11).

Redemption does not set us up and send us off to do our own thing. Instead, it brings us new responsibilities.

> *Do you not know that your body is the temple of the Holy Spirit who is in you, whom you have from God, and you are not your own? For you were bought at a price; therefore glorify God in your body and in your spirit, which are God's.* (1 Corinthians 6:19-20)

> *You were bought at a price; do not become slaves of men.* (1 Corinthians 7:23)

> *I beseech you therefore, brethren, by the mercies of God, that you present your bodies a living sacrifice, holy, acceptable to God, which is your reasonable service.* (Romans 12:1)

Like Onesimus, we are to be useful, not useless. We are not redeemed merely in our own interests. God has a wider purpose.

Responsibility is a privilege. Earlier, we saw how Redemption can be pictured as a marriage. A man and woman take on new responsibilities when they marry each other, but those responsibilities are a pleasure and privilege. The redeemed have the responsibility to serve the one they belong to – what a privilege and joy!

On a sea journey to Rome, Paul once testified to the entire ship's company that God was the one *to whom I belong and whom I serve* (Acts 27:23). The book of Revelation describes a countless multitude that have *washed their robes and made them white in the blood of the Lamb. Therefore they are before the throne of God, and serve Him day and night* (Revelation 7:14-15). The 'therefore' in this passage echoes the 'therefore' in Romans chapter twelve "*Therefore ... present your bodies a living sacrifice, holy, acceptable to God, which is your reasonable service.*"

## WITNESSES FOR GOD

Usefulness and service is one of God's promises to everyone who is redeemed. Life takes on direction and meaning. The reward for service is the privilege of greater service. If we serve God in small things, we will go on to serve Him in greater things, as Jesus said (Matthew 25:23). What is our service? As Jesus said, "*You shall be witnesses to Me*" (Acts 1:8).

Israel was redeemed not merely for their own sake, but to serve the whole world, to make known the name of the Lord. "*You are My witnesses,*" says the Lord (Isaiah 43:10). But they missed their national purpose. The Lord came looking for fruit from His vineyard, but found none. They tried to keep God to themselves and deeply resented any suggestion that He cared for non-Jews. They believed that the only way for non-Jews to know God was to become proselyte Jews.

Christians must not make this same mistake of keeping God to themselves. History must not be repeated. Jesus said: "*You will be my witnesses ... to the end of the earth*" (Acts 1:8). Could any responsibility be a greater privilege? Or more absorbing or satisfying? May we not repeat history and fail God!

# HOW CAN WE EXPERIENCE REDEMPTION?

## FROM DEATH TO LIFE

What is the purpose of Redemption? It is to deliver us from our godless ways to begin a new way of life. We looked at this quotation from one of Paul's letters earlier, but it is worth thinking about it again now:

> *Jesus Christ ... gave Himself for us, that He might redeem us from every lawless deed and purify for Himself His own special people, zealous for good works.* (Titus 2:13-14)

The purpose of Redemption is not fun, or a physical thrill, or tasting a supernatural experience. Most people live for the passing moment. Some people recite ritual chants as part of a quest for some kind of sensation, a feeling of inner tranquility and comfort. But Jesus had a far greater aim when He gave His life for us. It was not to gratify us with some kind of mystical experience – a drug can do that! Instead, God wants to begin an eternal work in our lives – to redeem us – and to do it now.

At the beginning of the Bible, God showed His readiness to help His people when He redeemed Israel from Egypt, from its slavery and idols. The Bible has always proclaimed a redeeming God, waiting to deliver us from all that holds us down and keeps us back.

At the coming of Jesus, He took the initiative and stepped into the world arena to fight for human freedom. At the cross, He gained for us eternal salvation and Redemption.

## WHAT WE NEED TO DO

All that the people of Israel had to do to receive their redemption was to walk out of Egypt. God made that possible. They had a lamb for their last meal, put its blood in a basin, and then painted it on their doorways. Because of this sign, destruction did not touch them during the final plague of judgment on Egypt. This was the first Passover (Exodus 12).

We, too, need to be prepared to leave 'Egypt' – to leave our old way of life, with its darkness, doubt, unbelief, godlessness, and sin. The contract that can set us free has already been signed, and the ransom has been paid. We can know Redemption from everything in our past when we repent and believe the Gospel.

Christ is our Lamb of God. His precious blood was poured out so that we can be saved from destruction. This second Passover takes us from death to life: *He who hears My word and believes in Him who sent Me has everlasting life, and shall not come into judgment, but has passed from death into life* (John 5:24).

The Bible says that *whoever calls on the name of the LORD shall be saved* (Joel 2:32). If you have never called on God, asking Him for your Redemption, you can use the prayer on the opposite page – now. As you pray to God, believe in your heart, and join the company of the millions on earth and in heaven who are the redeemed of the Lord.

*Dear heavenly Father,*

*I respond to Your invitation and come to You in the name of Your Son, Jesus Christ.*

*I come with all my sins, heartaches, and addictions.*

*I turn away from evil and turn to You, Lord Jesus.*

*I put my faith in You alone. You are the Son of the living God.*

*I believe with my heart what I now confess with my mouth: You are my Savior, my Lord, and my God.*

*Thank You for having accepted me as Your child. I open myself for Your Holy Spirit and will follow You all the days of my life. I believe You and receive You.*

*I pray in the name of Jesus.*

*Amen!*

# *First of all...* INTERCESSION

# FIRST OF ALL... INTERCESSION

*I exhort first of all that supplications, prayers, intercessions, and giving of thanks be made for all men.*
(1 Timothy 2:1)

## 1 – THE SILENT PLANET

Why do we need prayer? In the beginning, Adam and Eve did not pray in the sense in which most of us would understand prayer today. God and man seemed to enjoy almost family openness. God was the 'Voice' walking in the garden in the cool of the day.

Then the party broke up. Relations became strained and distant. C. S. Lewis described this world as 'the silent planet' – silent toward heaven. Earth hung in space like a spiritual black hole, which gave no light.

> *The LORD looks down from heaven upon the children of men, to see if there are any who understand, who seek God. They have all turned aside, they have together become corrupt; There is none who does good, No, not one.*
> (Psalm 14:2-3)

## ATTACK

Think of what happens to a country at war; in some cases it is totally cut off from the outside world. There is no more commerce or trade, no more mail or telephone conversations. Much the same thing happened when the human race surrendered to sin and the devil. We were cut off from the outside world – from God, and from the world of the Spirit. Demonic forces occupied this world and dominated our attitudes. Divine power lines were severed and a permanent spiritual blackout occurred.

Originally, God put man in charge to manage this world, but we were a pushover to sin, and the devil swayed people as Rasputin swayed the Czar of Russia. The Bible makes this clear:

> *The whole world lies under the sway of the wicked one.*
> (1 John 5:19)
>
> *(Our) foolish hearts were darkened.* (Romans 1:21)
>
> *The prince of the power of the air, the spirit who now works in the sons of disobedience.* (Ephesians 2:2)
>
> *Alienated and enemies in your mind by wicked works.* (Colossians 1:21)

Three times Jesus called the devil *"the ruler of this world"* (John 12:31, 14:30, 16:11). When the devil offered the kingdoms of this world to Christ, Jesus did not contest the devil's ability to do so (Matthew 4:8-9).

## COUNTERATTACK

God's wisdom permitted this state of affairs, because He had counter plans. Just as in wartime countries have secret agents and the means of maintaining contact with them, so the Lord had His men and women and kept in contact with them. Amos the prophet said, *"Surely the Lord GOD does nothing, unless He reveals His secret to His servants the prophets"* (Amos 3:7) – men like Enoch, Noah, Abraham, Moses, Elijah, Daniel, and Isaiah. The whole nation of Israel was to have been God's ally against the occupying enemy from hell, but they failed to perceive His plan and comply with it.

The Lord revealed one great secret to His servants the prophets, namely that there was to be an invasion of fortress Earth from the outside. It took place. Christ came to the shores of Satan's usurped dominion proclaiming the kingdom of God and displaying its power. *"But if I cast out demons with the finger of God, surely the kingdom of God has come upon you"* (Luke 11:20).

## STRATEGIC WEAPONRY

Christians have a world to reclaim and regain for God. The enemy has brought about vast destruction, death, and wickedness. Prayer opens up God's armory with its superior weapons. If we think that we do not need to pray, then we do not know what we are up against. If we think that we can manage on our own achievements, then we simply make ourselves the devil's laughing stock. Prayer-less means defenseless.

> *If we think that we do not need to pray, then we do not know what we are up against.*

Cleverness and science are like a feather duster against a tank. The unlimited greatness of the Cross is needed against the cosmic evil.

Prayer and intercession cast out the entrenched enemy, violate his borders, and retake lost territory. The devil hates this kind of prayer. It is heaven's militancy. It is not a muttered litany, but a top C soul-shriek. Prayer is an aggressive multipurpose weapon put in our hands by God to overcome every kind of satanic resistance. The man who prays overleaps human limits. Believers are authorized to go to the counter of heaven's supply-store for superhuman resources.

## THE NEW AND LIVING WAY

The coming of Christ was the beginning of the end for the devil. The spiritual advance goes on today. The armies of God form a new race of men and women, a holy nation, born again, presenting the Word of God with faith and prayer. We have new access to God, a new method of operation and new authority, *by a new and living way*, through Christ Jesus (Hebrews 10:20). Victory is assured.

> *The creation itself also will be delivered from the bondage of corruption into the glorious liberty of the children of God ... for we were saved in this hope.* (Romans 8:21, 24)

Why live as if we were not on speaking terms with the Lord? He dwells with us. We are not mere neighbors, living with a brick wall between us. The Lord has broken down the middle wall. We have been *brought near by the blood of Christ* (Ephesians 2:13). The Christian life means life with God, with everything centered on Him, God-orientated. The Holy Spirit gives us *utterance* to get through to God (Acts 2:4).

> *Why live as if we were not on speaking terms with the Lord?*

Christ's model prayer ends with – *For Yours is the kingdom and the power and the glory forever* (Matthew 6:13). His is the power, ours is the prayer. Prayer is necessary, not just nice – a vital part of the equation. Ezekiel the prophet pictures the currents of the Spirit as waters to swim in (Ezekiel 47). The Lord provides the waters, but we do the swimming. Without prayer, we are not 'in the swim' at all.

# 2 – ALL PRAYER

Turn over each page of the New Testament and mark every prayer reference. Then you will see how prayer is emphasized. In the first Gospel alone there are forty-one references and two hundred and thirty throughout the New Testament, some of them extensive, with ten different words for prayer. We read there about *praying always with* ALL *prayer* (Ephesians 6:18). There are different methods, forms, and moods, yet all of them available for man to use against the devil.

## KEEP PRAYING!

Some texts use one special word like a hammer to drive the nail in deep. The adverb 'without ceasing' (Greek *ektenes* = constant, *adialeiptos* = without ceasing) comes only six times in Scripture and only about prayer, as if this were the one thing never to let up.

> *Peter was therefore kept in prison, but* CONSTANT *prayer was offered to God for him by the church.* (Acts 12:5)

> WITHOUT CEASING *I make mention of you always in my prayers.* (Romans 1:9)

> *We give thanks to God always for you all, making mention of you in our prayers, remembering* WITHOUT CEASING *your work of faith.* (1 Thessalonians 1:2-3)

> *We also thank God* WITHOUT CEASING. (1 Thessalonians 2:13)

> *Pray* WITHOUT CEASING. (1 Thessalonians 5:17)

> WITHOUT CEASING *I remember you in my prayers night and day.* (2 Timothy 1:3)

Jesus Himself taught that *men always ought to pray and not lose heart* (Luke 18:1).

Another set of examples shows the use of a word meaning 'keep at it, persevere, be a stayer, show stamina, stick at it, keep awake!' Translate these texts like that yourself:

> CONTINUE EARNESTLY *in prayer, being vigilant in it with thanksgiving.* (Colossians 4:2)
>
> CONTINUING STEADFASTLY *in prayer.* (Romans 12:12)
>
> *We will give ourselves* CONTINUALLY *to prayer.* (Acts 6:4)
>
> *Praying* ALWAYS *with all prayer and supplication in the Spirit, being watchful to this end with all perseverance and supplication for all the saints.* (Ephesians 6:18)

The way that Jesus speaks of prayer is not quite like some suppose. He said, *"Ask, and it will be given to you. Seek. Knock"* (Matthew 7:7). These words are in the Greek present indicative – be asking, be seeking, be knocking. But elsewhere He used a different tense (aorist) indicating a single, completed action – *"Give us this day our daily bread"* (Matthew 6:11). Ask once, but every day, *"Give us this day."* Ask for each day's need daily. That is how God likes it, not 'having faith' for everything for a whole year, but coming to Him as children over and over, asking for the bread of life, and the Holy Spirit, daily, not once forever. We always receive every day.

## GOD HEARS PRAYER

Scripture consistently declares that prayer will always be heard.

> *Your Father knows the things you have need of before you ask Him.* (Matthew 6:8)

*Everyone who asks receives, and he who seeks finds, and to him who knocks it will be opened.* (Matthew 7:8)

*Now this is the confidence that we have in Him, that if we ask anything according to His will, He hears us. And if we know that He hears us, whatever we ask, we know that we have the petitions that we have asked of Him.* (1 John 5:14-15)

# 3 – FOLLOWING THE RULES

To pray, simply follow the ground rules. There are conditions attached, but none that are impossible to fulfill.

1. Ask in faith in God (Matthew 21:22; James 1:6). We cannot ask too much and blow a fuse by overloading the demand on divine help. "Ask!" That is Christ's command, so you cannot be outside the will of God by asking, but you can if you do not ask.

2. Do not come apologetically in case you are asking inappropriately or outside God's will. Our job is to ask anyway, and let God decide how to act. It will not upset God, whatever we ask. We can worry so much about God's will that we never have any faith at all or maybe never pray! We have made it such a mark of high piety to ask only for what God wants that it contradicts what Jesus said in John 15:7: *"Ask what you desire, and it shall be done for you."* God allows mature believers free choice over large areas of their lives – and blesses what they decide.

3. Forgive as God forgives you (Mark 11:25; Luke 6:37; Matthew 5:23-24).

4. Do not pray 'to be heard of men,' but sincerely – not as was said of one preacher "his prayer was the most eloquent ever delivered to a New York congregation." Remember God is full of grace (Luke 18:10-14).

5. Pray in the name of Jesus (John 14:13, 16:23). Since we are in Christ, one with Him, when we pray in the name of Jesus, we are speaking with Christ's merits imputed to us. Common sense says we cannot ask, "In the name of Jesus, help me to rob my neighbor!" Two women who wrote to a preacher overlooked this and said, "We are praying for your death. We have been successful in two previous cases!"

6. Cherish the Word of God. Notice the balance of this sentence: *If you abide in Me, and My words abide in you, you will ask what you desire, and it shall be done for you* (John 15:7). *If I regard iniquity in my heart, the Lord will not hear* (Psalm 66:18). Treasure the Word of Christ; do not cherish iniquity.

7. Deal with obstacles to answered prayer. James warns why many times we may not be heard. *But let him ask in faith, with no doubting, for he who doubts is like a wave of the sea driven and tossed by the wind. For let not that man suppose that he will receive anything from the Lord* (James 1:6-7). *You ask and do not receive, because you ask amiss, that you may spend it on your pleasures* (James 4:3).

## PERFECT WISDOM

Jesus prayed, *"not My will, but Yours, be done."* (Luke 22:42). We are not all-wise and do not make perfect petitions. If we had the management of omnipotence (unlimited power), we would soon make a mess of things. God, however, will not be persuaded to do what is folly – not even to please somebody. His answers are wiser than our prayers – even His "No's!"

It used to be taught that King Hezekiah (Isaiah 38) prayed for longer life, and God gave him another fifteen years, but against His will because during those fifteen years Manasseh, Hezekiah's son, was born and for over fifty years led the nation into wickedness. But in fact if Hezekiah had died without a son, the Davidic line to Christ as chronicled in Matthew chapter one would have come to a premature end. God does nothing against His will – pray on!

# 4 – KNOWING GOD

Above everything else, know the Lord. How easy it is to ask the wrong person for the things we need! But we do not usually ask a plumber for medicine or a doctor to repair a water pipe. Know who God is. Do not address a vague Somebody somewhere up in the stratosphere, with no idea of who He is or how He might react. Do not be like the liberal preacher who thought of God as 'a kind of oblong blur,' or like the Athenians with an altar to the unknown god (Acts 17:22-23). Some people even talk of "seeking the unknown."

That kind of mystical nonsense is like begging from any passer-by, hoping to chance on a billionaire. But it is better to know a billionaire. To recognize God's true identity always encourages more intelligent and more effective praying. God is our Father.

What kind of reaction can we expect if we treat God as an 'oblong blur'? The Almighty has made almighty efforts to tell us about Himself, even sending Jesus Christ. To ignore what He says involves a deliberate and dangerous resolution to remain in ignorance, exactly what we might expect when the devil influences us. To brush aside the greatest spiritual knowledge ever revealed is suicidal. Even God Himself can do nothing more for us then.

People question why, if God is all-powerful, He does not do this or that. But God is not only all-powerful, but also all-wise, holy, and just. Furthermore He has His own prior plans, not likely to be changed for one of our impulses. You do not ask a surgeon performing an operation to make you a cup of tea. We must at least flow in the direction of the divine stream.

## READ THE BIBLE

Know God, His ways, His counsel, His character! All His attributes are laid open in His Word. Read it! This is the secret of so many Christians' wonderful faith and confidence, their path to God guided by Scripture.

The book of James, largely about prayer, speaks of God's goodness as always shining like the sun.

> *Every good gift and every perfect gift is from above, and comes down from the Father of lights, with whom there is no variation or shadow of turning.* (James 1:17)

This picture is a sundial, which registers the sun's movement by its shadow. When there is no shadow, it is noon, because the sun is at the zenith and casts no shadow. God never casts a shadow because He is always at the zenith. He never varies, changes, or declines. For everybody, He is always the same prayer-answering God.

# 5 – THE NEW WAY

The first Christians crossed the Bible landscape in an aura of prayer. They reveled in prayer, and with good reason. Their kind of praying was a new thing, using the name of Jesus. The New Testament speaks of *fellowship with the Father,* but Israel did not pray "Our Father." They had such a lofty conception of God that He seemed unapproachable, the Sovereign Lord of Hosts, mighty in battle, or at best a present help in trouble.

Only an elite band enjoyed God's company and intimate prayer life with Him. Most knew God only second-hand, via a priest or prophet. In a sense, people called on the Lord in their own name. *Lord, remember David* (Psalm 132:1), hoping for personal favor.

## "OUR FATHER"

We should all seek to perceive God's true position; He is infinitely superior to us. But the invitation to call Him Father brings Him close to us and makes Him approachable. Readers of the book of Hebrews, still emerging from the old dispensation, had to be taken by the hand, and led into this new relationship. They were told:

> *Seeing then that we have a great High Priest ... Jesus the Son of God ... let us therefore come boldly to the throne of grace ... having boldness to enter the Holiest by the blood of Jesus, by a new and living way which He consecrated for us, through the veil, that is, His flesh.* (Hebrews 4:14-16, 10:19-20)

When Jesus taught His disciples to pray, it made them a new breed, praying always and about everything. He had told them, *"Most assuredly, I say to you, whatever you ask the Father in My name He will give you ... ask, and you will receive"* (John 16:23-24). In a way, to call on God is instinctive. Who does not – especially when in distress? But Christ taught us the right way to go about it – to pray in His name. His mighty works mark a new road to God. He has opened heaven's door. Enter! We will be received.

*Christ taught us the right way to pray – to pray in His name.*

# REVELING IN PRAYER

The quotations above are part of an astonishing New Testament array of similar references to prayer. The main word for prayer (Greek *proseuche, proseuchomai*) is used over one hundred and twenty times. God gives many things without being asked – rain, sunshine, winter, and summer – but He planned that we should receive other things by asking for them. The list is long and includes salvation, the Holy Spirit, guidance, equipment for spiritual battles, the Gifts of the Spirit, power to witness, strength, effectiveness, boldness, relief from anxieties, anti-devil weapons, our 'daily bread', the kingdom to come, the will of God to be done, relief from trial and temptation, healing – and more. We are even to pray for our enemies.

Communicating with God is the Christian distinctive. Jesus forbids *'vain repetition,'* like bowing five times a day declaring that God is great. The disciples opened their hearts to God about everything, including their innermost feelings. For example, they wrote letters in the style of those days but changed the usual good wishes and pleasantries into prayers. Paul wrote to Christians in Rome, "*Without ceasing, I make mention of you always in my prayers*" (Romans 1:9). To believers in Corinth, Galatia, Ephesus, Philippi, Colosse, Thessalonica, and to Timothy, he wrote: "*Grace to you and peace from God our Father and the Lord Jesus Christ.*" Some letters appear to be just extended prayers. Augustine wrote his immortal book 'Confessions' as a letter to God.

"If wishes were horses, beggars would ride," they say, but the first Christians addressed wishes to the Father in the name of Jesus and did ride. Praise God! The unbeliever wishes, the believer prays. In Acts 27:29, the soldiers and crew of a ship were in danger and 'wished for daybreak.' Paul prayed, and they were saved.

James 'wished' in the Christian way: "*Pray* (wish) *for one another that you may be healed*" (James 5:16). Like John writing to Gaius, "*I pray* (wish) *that you may prosper in all things and be in health*" (3 John 2). Wishes become prayers and answers are expected. The unbeliever sighs, "If only..." The believer rejoices *in hope of the glory of God* (Romans 5:2).

# 6 – INTERCESSION

Intercession is a special form of prayer for believers. But what exactly is involved in intercession?

## 1. A special assignment for believers

Believers are called to a special work, not just to ask for things for themselves but also to stand before God for others. This is a vital feature of the superstructure of world redemption. Christ is the 'Great Intercessor,' and we are called to a similar role. Christ's intercessory work is on a different level from ours, but He is still our role model.

## 2. Dual knowledge

Intercession needs knowledge of those for whom we intercede and of the One to whom we address our prayers. Jesus took our nature on Himself and also carried the nature of God in perfection – He was fully human and fully divine. He identified Himself with us and with God. We are human, but have received the *divine nature* (2 Peter 1:4). We have kinship with both God and man. And so we are fitted for the work to which God has appointed us.

### 3. Christ-like compassion

However, we need more if we are to enter into true intercession. Our role model, Jesus, poured out a flood of compassion. This was His sole motivating force. The effective power of intercession derives from a spontaneous outflow of concern and love. Generally speaking, it is naturally there for our own family and friends. Now, it must embrace all the world.

## SOME EXAMPLES

Although the Christian basis of prayer is not in the Old Testament, it is there that we find the great examples of intercession. Abraham interceded for Abimelech, and for the doomed cities of Sodom and Gomorrah. Moses, Solomon, Elijah, Hezekiah, Daniel, Ezra, Esther, Jeremiah, and the prophets interceded for the nation of Israel. There are even intercessory Psalms.

As an evangelist I am called to stand before very big crowds, but I dare not preach unless I know that intercessory prayer has ascended for those very people. Workers go out to the crusade area in advance and spend several weeks there, specifically to prepare the ground through intercession. Christians are recruited locally and instructed to storm heaven with pleadings for the souls of men and women. Indeed, when these teams of intercessors hammer on the door of glory, it adds weight to the prayers of tens of thousands of people around the whole world that the souls of those in the crowd may be delivered and saved.

During our evangelistic crusades, a spirit of prayer and intercession soaks my soul and often makes me jump out of bed at three o'clock in the morning. Hundreds, sometimes thousands, of intercessors uphold me in prayer while I am ministering on the platform.

This provides my spirit with lift like a powerful thermal for an eagle. I glance across a sea of faces and rejoice that the devil's hand has been struck off their shoulders.

In western churches, comparatively few unbelievers venture to expose themselves to evangelism. Usually, they are brought to a meeting by somebody who has sought God on their behalf – perhaps for years. The ground is already watered with tears and prepared. What about the teeming populations of Africa, Asia, China, India, Japan, and Indonesia? How many are ever named personally before the Lord? These great unprayed-for masses are struggling human beings like ourselves, however remotely acquainted we are with them. If we do not intercede for them, who will?

## LASER BEAMS

In the darkness of a bedeviled world, our prayers cut the darkness like lasers, becoming channels through which God's blessing may reach earth, and transmitting the power-currents of Calvary and the Resurrection. Intercession jams the wavelengths of the devil. Certainly the devil will resist and the world will howl in protest, too long undisturbed. The works of Satan are many, but they must go. *For this purpose the Son of God was manifested, that He might destroy the works of the devil* (1 John 3:8).

Intercession honors those for whom we pray, better than recommending them for the Honors List. In 2 Kings 4 we read about a great woman. She is called great, but she was not famous and did not want to be. She gave quiet hospitality to Elisha the prophet, and to thank her, he asked, *"Do you want me to speak on your behalf to the king or to the commander of the army?"* (2 Kings 4:13). "No!" she said. High circles did not attract her, but she did want Elisha to name her to God. He did so, and this began the thrilling miracle story of the birth of her son, his death, and his being raised to life again. Elisha named her to the Lord, and it brought her immortal fame.

Praying brings distinction to ourselves and to those for whom we pray. It highlights them, makes nobodies somebodies before God. He turns His attention to them – just imagine that! *I sought for a man among them who would make a wall, and stand in the gap before Me on behalf of the land, that I should not destroy it; but I found no one* (Ezekiel 22:30). Politicians, talkers, musicians, but not one intercessor. If He had found a man, his name would be in the Book, immortalized. To intercede means we join an elite company notable in heaven.

> *Intercession may be the only practical thing we can do for some people.*

It may be the only practical thing we can do for some people. Elisha could only pray for his hostess. To omit prayer from our activities is loveless, grieving the Spirit of God. Samuel looked at wayward · Israel and said, *"You have done all this wickedness ... far be it from me that I should sin against the LORD in ceasing to pray for you"* (1 Samuel 12:20, 23).

## HEART-CRY

To God, nobody is a nobody. Each individual has a value beyond computation. Our prayers should be in direct proportion to the desperate wickedness from which people need saving. The worse the wickedness, the more the intercession. No one should have to go through life without somebody praying for him (or her).

Let me ask you to read the following passage from 1 Timothy 2:1-4:

> *Therefore I exhort first of all that supplications, prayers, intercessions, and giving of thanks be made FOR ALL men,*

*for kings and all who are in authority, that we may lead a quiet and peaceable life in all godliness and reverence. For this is good and acceptable in the sight of God our Savior, who desires all men to be saved and to come to the knowledge of the truth.*

So, the ultimate aim of intercession is evangelism – God *desires all men to be saved.* Intercession is not a say-so, but a heart-cry. Not "Lord, bless me and everybody everywhere. Amen!" Our Lord Jesus prayed for us until He sweat drops of blood. He even prayed for the soldiers hammering nails through His quivering flesh.

Pray for all men, for Christlessness is terrible. There is only one Savior, and if He is rejected what can people do? Their cry is like Reuben's when he found Joseph had gone: *"And I, where shall I go?"* (Genesis 37:30). There is nowhere to go. So, people just drift along, perhaps together, unknowingly heading for a Sargasso Sea called hell. Christless religion is hell on earth. Religious leaders killed Christ. We see it today in unbridled hate, terrorism, murder, and oppression in the name of God. Jesus said, *"If you were Abraham's children, you would do the works of Abraham. But now you seek to kill Me ... Abraham did not do this. You are of your father the devil ... he was a murderer from the beginning"* (John 8:39 44). Intercession is urgent. Intercession brings divine intervention. We have one generation in which to save a generation, not a century.

> *We have one generation in which to save a generation, not a century.*

Alfred Lord Tennyson only told half the truth when he wrote, "More things are wrought by prayer than this world dreams of." The other half is this – more things are not handled in prayer than this world dreams of. We live dangerously, leaving many important matters out of our prayers.

Unanswered prayers are usually the ones that were never prayed, but interceding for the salvation of the nations receives immediate attention. It touches the heart-interest of God.

# 7 – HOW TO BECOME A TRUE INTERCESSOR

1. A true intercessor must have some standing with both parties.

As I have already written, we know people, but we must also know God! Abraham is a good example of someone who knew God. The cities of Sodom and Gomorrah had become morally perverted so God proposed to remove them. He said, *"Shall I hide from Abraham what I am doing?"* (Genesis 18:17) When Abraham learned that these two cities were listed for destruction, he took up their case with God and went a long way along the road to saving them. He was qualified because he knew God – and the cities.

> *Abraham was a qualified intercessor because he knew God – and the cities.*

He was called the friend of God (2 Chronicles 20:7; Isaiah 41:8). Why? *Abraham believed God, and it was accounted to him for righteousness. And he was called the friend of God* (James 2:23). Believers – I do not mean unbelieving believers full of doubts, asking clever questions, but men and women of living faith, who know the Lord – are the King's friends at court, His confidants, people to whom He listens and with whom He wants to cooperate. They are to be His intercessors.

That is what Scripture means by a friend. Jesus said, *"No longer do I call you servants ... but I have called you friends, for all things that I heard from My Father I have made known to you*" (John 15:15). A friend-intercessor will have the mind of the Lord, who tells us nothing for mere interest but for us to pray about it. A word of knowledge is not necessarily for public consumption but for private prayer. God reveals what He will do to those who clamor for His will to be done.

After a campaign meeting a lady came to me and told me how she had been "molested by evil spirits for very many years" and how she despaired of life. I was moved by what she said, and I promised to pray for her. When I reached my hotel, the Lord told me to fast and pray for her. I did so. The next day I was praying for her with all of my heart, when at noon I suddenly experienced a breakthrough. The glory of the Lord filled my soul and the Holy Spirit said to me, "It is done." That evening I met the lady again. Before I could say anything, she said with shining eyes, "God has done the miracle. Today at noon, I experienced a mighty deliverance at my home." What God does on a small scale, he will also do on the largest.

> *A word of knowledge is not necessarily for public consumption but for private prayer.*

## 2. A true intercessor is moved by feelings of concern.

The story in Exodus 32 is a strange episode, but shows us the heart of a true intercessor. Moses was angry over Israel's idolatry. Israel had escaped from Egypt after a fantastic display of omnipotence that would make God seem physically near. Above them towered Mount Sinai, with the cloud of God's glory concealing Moses, who had ascended to speak with God. The people thought he had deserted them. Their simple minds were soaked in the superstitions of Egypt and its gods, and so they made a golden calf to lead them back to Egypt.

The Lord said He would put an end to them because of this appalling lapse and begin a new nation through Moses. Moses' first reaction

*Moses offered to die as an atonement for Israel's sin. This is true · intercession.*

was to send swordsmen to rid Israel of the ringleaders. Then his pity overcame his anger and he besought God to save the nation God called *"a stiff-necked people"* (Exodus 32:9). Moses called them *"Your people"* (verse 11) and pleaded, *"Oh, these people have committed a great sin ... yet now, if You will forgive their sin – but if not, I pray, blot me out of Your book which You have written".* (Exodus 32:31-32). Here words failed him, such was the force of his compassionate outburst. He offered to die as an atonement for Israel's sin. His offer was turned down because only the Son of God could atone for sin. But this is an example of true intercession.

This proposal was unsolicited. Moses had not been pushed into it. He had brought this rabble of tribes to nationhood like a woman bringing a child into the world. They broke his heart, but he still defended them from the inevitable disaster of their own folly.

We pray for Christian revival. Why? To see the church full, pay the bills, ease the labors of evangelism, as a religious duty? Look at the pitiful attempts of Christless people to save themselves, making their own impotent gods. Let us weep for them. Let us cry out to God (Joel 1:13-14, 2:12-13). God is moved when our hearts – not just our mouths – are moved.

### 3. A true intercessor has faith.

All the great prayers of intercession in Scripture were triggered heavenward from the launch pad of faith. Faith is assurance of the changeless character of God's goodness, believing He is faithful to what He says He is. If prayer is controversial, then everything is. If all answers to prayer were printed, they would fill the Atlantic depths.

Faith is faith in GOD, not just in a miracle happening. The great Bible intercessors did not always see what they asked for. God heard Abraham, but in the end the cities of Sodom and Gomorrah were destroyed. Pray on and leave matters in God's hands to do whatever He knows is good.

## 4. A true intercessor delights in praise and worship.

Throughout the intercessory Psalms, there is not a single instance of honor to God being omitted in some shape or form. The one psalm of unrelieved gloom, Psalm 88, makes no petition and offers no praise. But intercession rises to God on the wings of worship. Requests and praise are two sides of the same coin.

> *Be anxious for nothing, but in everything by prayer and supplication, with thanksgiving, let your requests be made known to God.* (Philippians 4:6)

> *As you have therefore received Christ Jesus the Lord, so walk in Him ... abounding in it with thanksgiving. Continue earnestly in prayer, being vigilant in it with thanksgiving.* (Colossians 2:6-7, 4:2)

> *Rejoice always, pray without ceasing, in everything give thanks; for this is the will of God in Christ Jesus for you.* (1 Thessalonians 5:16-18)

> *Let the hearts of those rejoice who seek the LORD!* (Psalm 105:3)

Intercessors do not come to God being offended about what He has not done. Moaning is not praying. Our burden for the world's needs is lifted as we pray in remembrance and thanks for what He can – and will – do.

The Lord's Prayer begins *"Our Father ... hallowed be Your name."* That is the beginning of all true intercession, and the end is *" for Yours is the kingdom and power and the glory for ever and ever. Amen."*

∽

# Faith for the Night

# FAITH FOR THE NIGHT

## THE FAITH FACTOR

The Bible was written for people with no real faith. Faith is not 'believing what you know is not true,' nor 'believing something for which there is no evidence.' That is foolishness.

If we have no faith, reading the Bible produces it, and if we have some faith, we get more the same way. There's no mystique about it. We are born believers, having faith every day in our doctors and bankers, in our spouses and bosses. Without this natural faith, we could not function. Faith is possible to everybody.

Of course, people say, "Seeing is believing." But if you can prove it, faith is unnecessary! Not seeing is no reason for not believing. Nobody sees radiation, but we know its effects. Nobody sees God, but millions see His effect in their lives. Faith is a decision.

## THE FAITH FUSE

Faith has neither bulk nor weight, for it is what you do. Jesus spoke of *faith as a mustard seed* (Luke 17:6), referring to something tiny with huge potential. Perhaps today, he might speak of faith as a fuse. Tiny as it is, it transmits the awesome power generated in power stations to our homes. Without it, every appliance is useless, unable to draw from that power.

As believers, we know what we believe and Who we believe. Believing tests us. Taking God's Word at face value, accepting its divine authority, we plug into the very source! Faith is the vital link. By it, the energies of Heaven flow into the world. The greatness of God, of the work of Christ, of the Word of God are all there, but without faith, as small as a fuse wire, none of that greatness avails. The circuit is broken. But once connected, the fuse shows the effects of the power surging through it. It warms up! Faith makes us dynamic, exuberant, and excited!

## FAITH THE GOLDEN GIFT

Faith in Christ is different to any other kind of faith. It is not found in the Old Testament. In the New Testament, the word used means believing 'into' Christ, suggesting movement. Faith IN Christ means moving close to Him in trustful love. It is an embrace.

This kind of loving embrace between man and his Maker comes only through Christ. Nobody in the Old Testament days could think of such a thing. God was spirit, another kind of being, too awesome to be approached except with fear and trembling. Yet one inspired book in the Old Testament Scriptures touches the heart of a new experience – the Song of Songs, a lyric of love that gathers up all its words of supreme love in one phrase, *I am my beloved's, and my beloved is mine.* (Song of Songs 6:3). This was an attitude towards God that nobody understood, until Christ came.

> *This kind of loving embrace between man and his Maker comes only through Christ.*

Faced with His reality, ordinary people in the Gospel suddenly knew He was the Savior, a swift revelation followed by complete commitment. No longer was faith for the rare individual, as in the Old Testament. Somehow, Calvary does what the awesome manifestations of Sinai could not do. Jesus is the great faith-creator. He said Himself, *"No one comes to the Father except through Me"* (John 14:6). He does not point to a way. Christ IS the way.

## A PRESENT-TENSE FAITH

A leper in the New Testament saw something about Christ that few others have. Meeting Jesus, he said, *"Lord, if You are willing, You can make me clean."* (Matthew 8:2). Not 'If you can, you will,' but 'If you will, you can!' The Bible was not written to tell us what God CAN do. We know God is Almighty. The Bible tells us what He WILL do.

It is easy to believe that God did things long ago. But past-tense faith is hollow unless it transfers to today. John wrote of faith in three tenses; past, present and future. He said: *"Grace to you and peace from Him who is and who was and who is to come ... and from Jesus Christ, the faithful witness"* (Revelation 1:4-5). What He will be, He is now and always has been!

The God who created the universe did not go into retirement when it was done! What He did then shows us what He is now, and always will be – creative, active, and good. Creation was the first and greatest of all miracles. What is the problem with God healing deaf ears or blind eyes? Yet many have a used-to-be God, anchored in history.

> *The Bible was not written to tell us what God can do. The Bible tells us what He will do.*

Unbelief sees today's miracles as suspect. Bible miracles were real, but today's are spurious. Today's tongues cannot be the same as at Pentecost. God answered prayer then, but now it is coincidence. What does Jesus reply to this pessimism? *"If you would believe you would see the glory of God"* (John 11:40).

## BREAKTHROUGH FAITH

The dynamic of faith is that as we act, God acts. People often pray, 'use me, O Lord,' but do nothing. You cannot wait to 'feel' faith, for it is not a feeling. You simply do what should be done when you know that you cannot succeed unless God helps you. The whole Bible is written to break down unbelief and build up our trust in God. Here are a few 'breakthrough' Bible verses.

> *Do not be conformed to this world, but be transformed by the renewing of your mind.* (Romans 12:2)

> *If you would believe you would see the glory of God.* (John 11:40)

> *Abraham believed God, and it was accounted to him for righteousness. And he was called the friend of God.* (James 2:23)

> *Forgetting those things which are behind and reaching forward to those things which are ahead, I press toward the goal for the prize of the upward call of God in Christ Jesus.* (Philippians 3:13-14)

We talk of 'big believers' with 'great faith.' But some event inspired them and encouraged them. They took their opportunity, changed their attitude, and believed faith is a leap into the light, not into the darkness. Believing is like a child standing where it is not safe but without any fear because its father is waiting to catch him. He falls on purpose to be caught. Jesus never commended people, He commended their faith.

## TRUE FAITH

True faith means to place confidence in something. It is neither irrational, nor 'blind.' People the world over are putting their faith in countless religions, theories, sects and cults, the vast majority of which promise nothing this side of eternity. We are commonly told, 'Keep an open mind. Never be dogmatic.' What use is that? Do passengers want a pilot who is 'open-minded' about flying and his destination? It is not arrogance to be sure that the sun will rise in the morning. In the same way, Christians are sure of Christ and His promises.

> *The fact is, nobody understands what it is like to meet Jesus until they do.*

Unbelief about God is forgivable if people are ignorant about Him. But how can God forgive those who know He sent his Son to die for them, and yet will not listen? *How shall we escape if we neglect so great a salvation?* (Hebrews 2:3). The fact is, nobody understands what it is like to meet Jesus until they do.

## FAITH AND THE PROMISES OF GOD

Faith is the only basis for a workable relationship. We trust someone because we know him, and it is the Bible that shows us who God is. He has given us His word, making 7,874 promises in the Bible! Many of these are unsolicited, like: *While the earth remains, seedtime and harvest, cold and heat, winter and summer, and day and night shall not cease* (Genesis 8:22). Others are obtainable only by direct application. *Ask and you shall receive* (John 16:24).

The exercise of faith in prayer is a healthy activity, reminding us of our dependency on God. Through prayer, God makes us His co-workers. We ask, and THEN He performs. He planned this co-operation!

*Whatever you ask in My name, that I will do, that the Father may be glorified in the Son* (John 14:13). This promise is for the fulfillment of Christ's will.

We speak to God in prayer, and God speaks to us any time He wants.

> **We speak to God in prayer, and God speaks to us any time He wants.**

God reveals His will to all of us – we do not need to pry it out of Him. The aim of prayer is to bring us into line with His will, and then He hastens to answer. We cannot twist God's arm by fasting, or impressive numbers of intercessors. As James said, *"You do not have because you do not ask. You ask and do not receive, because you ask amiss, that you may spend it on your pleasures"* (James 4:2-3). If our heart is wrong, we get no answer.

## DEGREES OF FAITH

The ancients, like Enoch, Abraham, and Samuel, were men who knew God. Their stories give us vital guidance, showing faith to be a daily practical reliance. In the New Testament, this trust is continued and expanded. Jesus showed us that the state of our real self, our soul, was all-important.

Faith may follow a process like this:

- Believing something is true. Believing that there is a God is not enough (the devils believe the same thing James 2:19) but it is a start.

- Believing a person is genuine. Many believe that Jesus was a good man. But He claimed to be much more. He claimed to be the Savior of the world!

- Believing in Jesus as an inspired person, like a prophet. A prophet must be heard, and to hear Christ takes us a long way.

- Believing in God's power. Many believed in Christ's healing power, but did not make Him Lord and Savior.

- Believing as trust. Trust makes faith personal. We trust people we feel will not fail us.

- Believing in Christ. This is the real faith. It is complete surrender, letting Him take over every area of our lives.

## FAITH OF ABRAHAM

Faith changes those that change the world. Abraham was the first man noted for the 'obedience of faith.' Because of his faith, his name is inscribed on world history to this day. He did not believe out of tradition (there was none) or for a future hope. He simply walked by faith in God. Hebrews 11:10 says that *he waited for the city which has foundations, whose builder and maker is God.* He had a new vision, totally unlike the bloodthirsty times he lived in. Abraham knew little of the world, but he knew what life was all about. When God spoke to him, telling him to leave Ur of the Chaldees, off he went, not knowing where he was to go.

Why did God ask Abraham to sacrifice Isaac? God never meant Isaac to die, but was testing Abraham on his own cultural level. Abraham showed incredible faith in his obedience. As we read in Hebrews, he believed that God could raise Isaac from the dead if necessary. But God stayed his hand, and demonstrated a new culture in which bloodshed had no place.

Not only did Abram become Abraham, (the father of a multitude), but God then called Himself, *"the God of Abraham."* Faith relates us to God! Jesus said, *"Whoever confesses Me before men, him I will also confess before My Father who is in heaven"* (Matthew 10:32).

## FAITH AND THE NAMES OF GOD

There are many divine names in the Bible, and each one highlights a part of God's character. In Matthew 3:11, Jesus is indicated by the name-phrase, *He will baptize you with the Holy Spirit and fire.* This exciting phrase shows Him to be the God who spoke through Joel, saying, *"I will pour out My Spirit on all flesh"* (Joel 2:28).

Each of the Yahweh titles was given by revelation, opening up the mystery of God and giving us grounds for ever-increasing faith. Here are some of the riches revealed to us in this way:

- *Yahweh Sabaoth* – The Lord of Hosts.

  1 Samuel 7:45. God is on the side of His people in battle.

- *Yahweh-Jirah* – The Lord provides.

  Genesis 22:14. This partly fulfilled Abraham's prophecy that God would provide a lamb in Isaac's place, but the real fulfillment came when God provided the Lamb for the sins of the whole world, Jesus.

- *Yahweh Rophi* – The Lord heals.

  Exodus 15:26.

- *Yahweh-Nissi* – The Lord is my banner.

  Exodus 17:15. He is the God of victory.

- *Yahweh-Shalom* – The Lord is peace.

  Judges 6:24. Shalom spells out well-being, prosperity, good health, and safety.

- *Yahweh-Tsidkenu* – The Lord our righteousness.

  Jeremiah 23:6. This is spoken prophetically of the One to come, Jesus.

- *Yahweh Shammah* – The Lord is there.

  Ezekiel 48:35. He never arrives, but is always there. We cannot precede Him. Jesus said, *"For where two or three are gathered together in My name, I am there in the midst of them"* (Matthew 18:20).

Such YAHWEH titles could be multiplied, for the Lord is all things to all men. The principle is: *According to your faith let it be to you.* Will His names ever be exhausted?

## THE 'I WILL' GOD

The phrase, 'I will,' occurs about four thousand times in Scripture, and God says it far more than everybody else put together! In the New Testament, almost everything is said by Jesus, and He says constantly what He will do. Christ came to fulfill the Father's 'I will.' Therefore, His will is supreme. When Jesus said, *"I will,"* to the leper, it showed what kind of will it was. His will is good, merciful, and positive. And the Bible declares God's

> *He is a God of activity, unlike countless other gods, who do nothing.*

eternal will. There would be little point in telling us what His will was if it was not the same any more. We know God by what He DOES. He is a God of activity, unlike countless other gods, who do nothing. To have faith in God means to have faith in a God who acts.

When God says, 'I will,' it forms a covenant.

*Then God spoke to Noah and to his sons with him, saying:
"And as for Me, behold, I establish My covenant with you
and with your descendants after you, and with every living
creature that is with you." (Genesis 9:8, 10)*

This is a solo resolution, and unconditional. God's 'I will' covenants are spontaneous and absolute. Nobody pressed God for them, and they stand firm unconditionally.

Most of Christ's claims relate to the immediate present. He said, *"Come unto me ... and I WILL give you rest"* (Matthew 11:28). *"I will make you fishers of men"* (Matthew 4:19). There is a tremendous 'I will' in John 14:16, *"I will pray the Father, and He will give you another Helper."* The Day of Pentecost was an unsolicited act of the divine will. The disciples did not ask Him to do it. He said He would, and He did. He said, *"I will build My church"* and He has. He is doing so now, and He will complete it.

## KNOWING MEANS TRUSTING

Scripture hammers it home that we can trust God because of Who He is.

Why do we have faith in a person? We may believe what people say, but we believe in someone whom we consider to have integrity. Who we believe in is all-important. Jesus said, *"You believe in God, believe also in Me"* (John 14:1). *"He who believes in Me, believes not in Me but in Him who sent Me"* (John 12:44). Note the repeated 'Me.' God emphasizes the personal pronoun to encourage us to have confidence in Him because of His divine integrity. He says, 'I' over and over, *"I, even I, am the LORD" "I am He"* (Isaiah 43:11, 25; 41:4; 46:4). He wants us to trust Him for what He can do. *"Thus says the LORD, your Redeemer"* (Isaiah 3:14). If we do not trust Him, there's nobody else. *"There is no other name under heaven given among men by which we must be saved"* (Acts 4:12).

Isaiah 41:4 says, *"I, the LORD ... I [am] He."* Translators put in the verb 'am,' but God is actually speaking of Himself as 'I – He.' Now look at Zechariah 12:10, *they will look on Me whom they pierced. Yes, they will mourn for Him as one mourns for his only son.* So, 'Me' is the same One as 'Him' whom they pierced. It is the wonder-mystery of the Godhead. Since God is 'I am,' His Son is also, 'I am.' Jesus uses 'I am' in the absolute sense in John 8:58, *"Most assuredly, I say to you, before Abraham was, I AM."* He is the timeless One.

## FAITH FOR THE NIGHT

John 6 tells a well-known story. *It was already dark, and Jesus had not come to them. ... His disciples had gone away alone* (John 6:17, 22). The disciples were out on the lake, a dozen hardened fishermen – but without Jesus, they were 'alone'! Then Jesus, approaching on the water, calms their fears, saying, *"It is I; do not be afraid."* The words in the Greek are literally 'I am.' Because HE IS, we can feel safe. *Then they willingly received Him into the boat, and immediately the boat was at the land where they were going* (John 6:21). When Jesus arrived, they arrived!

> *Jesus is the light of the world. Without light, how can you find anything?*

Jesus is the only light of the world. If you follow any light, where do you find yourself? At the light! Some invite us to join their search for truth, but without light, how can they find anything? Paul warned us about blind guides who are *always learning and never able to come to the knowledge of the truth* (2 Timothy 3:7).

In fact, light and darkness are a constant theme of the Gospel of John. Its course is set in 1:5 – *And the light shines in the darkness, and the darkness did not comprehend it.* The word for 'comprehend' can be read as overtake, grasp, surprise, overcome and similar meanings. So many nuances – but however you read it, darkness cannot prevail against light. Faith is our infrared sight in the darkness, making visible the invisible.

## FROM FAITH TO FAITH

In John 9, Jesus noticed a blind man as He was leaving the temple. All the disciples could do was to ask the usual questions. Was he blind because of his own sin, or his parents? Jesus said, *"Neither this man nor his parents sinned, but that the works of God should be revealed in him."* He proceeded to heal him, demonstrating God's good nature. Then He turned the miracle into a parable. *"We must work the works of Him who sent Me, as long as it is day; night is coming, when no man can work. While I am in the world, I am the light of the world."* We must do the work of the One who sent Christ, bringing light and sight.

> *Faith is our infrared sight in the darkness, making visible the invisible.*

When the once-blind man was first asked who had healed him, he replied, *"A Man called Jesus"* (John 9:11). Asked again, he said, *"He is a prophet."* His faith was exploring the miracle. But the religious leaders wanted something to use against Christ, and tried to get him to say that Jesus was a sinner. He came right back with the one thing he had – his experience, *"though I was blind, now I see."* Pushed again, he spoke a truth that frightened them.

*Now we know that God does not hear sinners; but ...
since the world began it has been unheard of that anyone
opened the eyes of one who was born blind. If this Man
were not from God, He could do nothing.* (John 9:31-33).

At that, they threw him out! He had come a long way, and knew
that Jesus was 'from God.' Then Jesus found him, and asked,
*"Do you believe in the Son of God?"* His answer was, *"Lord, I believe!"*
And *he worshiped Him.* Faith has an ultimate purpose – life, and an
ultimate reaction, worship.

## FAITH IN THE NAME OF JESUS

*God also has highly exalted Him and given Him the name which is
above every name* (Philippians 2:9-11). All that is shown by the names
of the Lord (such as Yahweh-Jirah) is included in the name of Jesus.
*There is no other name under heaven given among men by which we
must be saved* (Acts 4:12). Hebrews 1:3 states He was *the express image*
of God's Being. God the Son means God the Father. When we
believe in the name of Jesus, we believe all that is in it.

Why was He given this name? It was a common Hebrew name
– Yeshua. To be one of us and one with us, He took on human nature
and a human name. The meaning of Jesus is 'The Lord (is) salvation.'
His name fulfilled the prophecy hidden in Isaiah 62:11, *"Say to the
daughter of Zion, 'Surely your salvation is coming"* or 'your yeshua is
coming.' Jesus means Savior.

Christ taught His disciples to pray (Matthew 6:6-15, Luke 11:1-4)
without making them say, 'in the name of Jesus.' Yet, He stresses
prayer in His name (John 14:14, 16:23). We are told to do everything,
*in the name of the Lord Jesus* (Colossians 3:17). This tells us that
saying the phrase, 'in the name of Jesus' is not essential. When we
minister to others, we do it with Christ, on His behalf. That is what

'in Jesus' name' means. What Christ showed us was brand new, for no one had ever prayed *in* the Lord's name before He came.

Lastly, prayer in Jesus' name is always to make the will of God possible. There is power in His name in that way. Repeating it over and over again as if it were a magic word will not coerce God to do what we want. Furthermore, praying does not create God's presence. We pray because God *is* present.

## THE PRAYER OF FAITH

Faith without prayer is possible. In fact, in Acts 3, Peter and John were going to pray, and healed a cripple on the way without praying

> **Prayer in Jesus' name is always to make the will of God possible.**

for him. But prayer without faith is useless. Jesus said, "*Whatever things you ask when you pray, believe that you receive them, and you will have them*" (Mark 11:24). Once we have believed can we stop praying? Is it unbelief to pray again? No! The prayer of faith sets up a faith-situation, and you stay in it until the prayer is answered. *Pray without ceasing* (1 Thessalonians 5:17), means 'Do not quit!'

The Book of James gives two examples of persistent believing and praying (James 5:7-8, 11, 17-18). Elijah was one, waiting in trust for the rain he had prophesied. And the other was Job. The 'patience of Job' was not with his sufferings, about which he had much to say, but with God. He never showed a flicker of mistrust in God. Romans 12:12 says that we should be *rejoicing in hope, patient in tribulation, continuing steadfastly in prayer.*

## FAITH AND FEAR

There are two kinds of fear, and both are in Exodus 20:20. *Do not fear; for God has come to test you, and that His fear may be before you, so that you may not sin.* The fear of God is good, a wholesome respect for His greatness, and it makes us godly. Without it, there is no restraint on evil. We either fear God, or we fear everything else, for we fear whatever seems greater than ourselves.

> *We either fear God, or we fear everything else.*

In the New Testament, the word for fear is usually *'phobeo.'* Jesus said, "Do not have phobia, have faith." Once or twice, another word is used, *'deilos,'* which means timidity or cowardice. *God has not given us a spirit of fear, but of power and of love and of a sound mind* (2 Timothy 1:7). Fear and worry are killers, but faith is the antidote! *Do not be afraid; only believe* (Luke 8:50).

Faith is not feeling. In the worst circumstances, faith frees us from fear's paralyzing effects. We overcome.

## FAITH AND THE DEVIL

Ever since Satan rose up wanting the honors of God (Isaiah 14:12-15), his aim has been domination. Humans must have seemed an easy target to him, but in God's eternal scheme, *God has chosen the weak things of the world to put to shame the things which are mighty* (1 Corinthians 1:27). Satan continues with his aims to this day. Among his strategies is the occult with all its manifestations. Against all these dangers, the Christian carries the bullet-proof shield of faith. Of course, Satan will try to rob us of that shield, for without faith, we are open to deadly personal damage.

There are Christians who seem more demon-conscious than Jesus-conscious. Satan loves to distract us with demon manifestations. But neither exorcism nor healing is the whole Gospel. We follow the example of Jesus in such things, and His mission was the kingdom of God. Jesus gave us a warning, too; *"Nevertheless do not rejoice in this, that the spirits are subject to you, but rather rejoice because your names are written in heaven"* (Luke 10:20). Actually, the occult is not the 'root of all evil.' *The love of money is a root of all evil* (1 Timothy 6:10). 1 Peter 5 echoes this and tells us to, *"Resist him,* [the Devil] *steadfast in the faith"* The battle is in us. We overcome the devil by guarding ourselves with the shield of faith, throwing our trust upon God, giving the devil no place in our lives. *This is the victory that has overcome the world, our faith* (1 John 5:4).

## MY GOD

Faith is the passport and visa into the kingdom and all its resources. It is not by the rules of any organization. If church members begin to bow to a leader's personal orders, it is a creeping death – cultism. Twice Jesus said, *"One is your Teacher, the Christ"* (Matthew 23:8, 10). Yet even He never interfered with the ordinary decisions of His disciples. The original word, 'disciple' in Scripture means 'learner' or 'follower,' and has nothing to do with discipline. His only rule was, *He who is not with Me is against Me* (Luke 11:23). Cultism is elitist, exclusive, while Jesus and the Gospel are all embracing.

> **Faith is the passport and visa into the kingdom and all its resources.**

We can all come by faith, and we are all instantly recognized by name. *Israel My elect, I have even called you by your name; I have named you, though you have not known Me* (Isaiah 45:4). Scripture constantly shows God dealing with individuals. Not only that, but He chooses us. Jesus said, *"You did not choose Me, but I chose you and appointed you"* (John 15:16). We belong to Him when He calls us and when we believe. For each individual, there is a unique contact with God. Each one who believes knows God in a way that no one else does!

> *We were made by Him and for Him in an intimate, personal way.*

God's greatness cannot be displayed through one life. It needs all our lives. The goodness of God is a great jewel with a million facets – together we display the wonders of His grace. We were made by Him and for Him in an intimate, personal way. God is MY God, just as He was the God of Abraham. Yahweh is Lord for every personality. We should not try to be a Paul, or Wesley, or Wigglesworth. Everyone believes God his way, according to God's plan.

## GOD'S PRESENCE

*I am the Alpha and the Omega, the Beginning and the End,"says the Lord, "who is and who was and who is to come, the Almighty* (Revelation 1:8). The words, *who is to come*, hold two blessings; that Jesus is coming again, and that God moves towards us all the time, with constant currents of blessing and power. His coming – in both senses – is given the name *'Parousia'* in the Bible, and means 'presence.' God never 'visits' us; I AM is always there. We are constantly in His presence, not just when we pray. Jesus made this clear when He promised, *"I will never leave you nor forsake you"* (Hebrews 13:5).

In John 14:18, Jesus says, *"I will come to you."* It is the present tense, 'I am coming to you,' and He includes the Father and Holy Spirit in verse 23; *"If anyone loves Me, he will keep My word; and My Father will love him, and We will come to him and make Our home with him."* That present coming is happening all over the world. It is not a case of God waking up one day and starting to do things. He waits only for us to dare and do in His name by faith. *"My Father has been working until now, and I have been working"* (John 5:17).

## ACTION!

Faith, like wiring, carries power, but is not power. It links us to the power source, God in heaven. Many people seek power, through thousands of theories and methods. Some Christian believers also seek the power of God by dubious processes, like extra-long prayer, or touching 'sacred' relics. But the mystic realms are not where disciples find power. It is available on earth. Christ's death and resurrection made available all the divine power we could ever need. It is the simple faith of ordinary people that touches Christ, not mysterious spirituality. Christ said, *"I am the way, the truth, and the life. No one comes to the Father except through Me"* (John 14:6). *There is one God and one Mediator between God and men, the Man Christ Jesus* (1 Timothy 2:5), and for that office, He paid the infinite price. Christ's final cry on the cross was, *"It is finished"* (John 19:30); His work was completed, perfected.

Hebrews 6:1 and 9:14 speak of *dead works* – good works not proceeding from faith. And James 2:26 gives the other side – *faith without works is dead*. If you never place yourself in a position where you must depend on God, your faith is meaningless. Deeds come alive with faith, and faith comes alive with deeds.

> *Therefore we also, since we are surrounded by so great a cloud of witnesses, let us lay aside every weight, and the sin which so easily ensnares us, and let us run with endurance the race that is set before us, looking unto Jesus, the author and finisher of our faith.* (Hebrews 12:1-2)

✧

*Winning your*

FRIENDS AND FAMILY

*to Christ*

# WINNING YOUR FRIENDS AND FAMILY TO CHRIST

*"I will pour My Spirit on your descendants,*
*and My blessing on your offspring.*
*One will say, 'I am the Lord's;'*
*another will call himself by the name of Jacob."*

Isaiah 44:3, 5

*"Blessed is the man who fears the Lord,*
*who delights greatly in His commandments.*
*His escendents will be mighty on earth;*
*the generation of the upright will be blessed.*
*Wealth and riches will be in his house,*
*and his righteousness endures for ever."*

Psalm 112:1-3

# WINNING YOUR FRIENDS AND FAMILY TO CHRIST

## SALVATION CREATES GODLY DYNASTIES

Those family trees, lists of names, at the beginning of the book of Numbers and Matthew's Gospel (and therefore the New Testament) may well put off many readers of the Bible. However, those daunting passages are vital to an understanding of how God sees things. They are wonderful evidence that we human beings matter, an indication of the immense value that God places on earthly kinships, from one generation to another.

Scripture uses the word "father" one thousand seven hundred times, "son" two thousand two hundred times, "family" four hundred times, "house and household" two thousand six hundred times, and has two thousand references to children, amounting to nearly nine thousand allusions to family life – one in every eighty-two words in the Bible. From a statistical perspective alone, it suggests that God is "in His element" in families and with His children. When people are saved, godly dynasties are created.

## THE LOOM OF CREATION

God has relations – children. He is a family God. The only true way we can relate to Him is as children of the Father. Jesus, who came to show us what God was like, never called God anything other than "Father."

What God is makes the world what it is. The Father's nature is reflected in the whole of life. The Father makes fathers. He has patterned everything after Himself – a fact which surfaces in nature and in family ties. All people on earth are probably related to each other as distant cousins. DNA science reveals that we have a pair of common ancestors. *"We are His people, and the sheep of His pasture"* (Psalm 100:3). On the loom of creation family relationships were woven into the very fabric of life.

## THE SOURCE OF THE FAMILY

The Trinity is the source of the family. The Father and the Son love each other and the Holy Spirit is the spirit of love in the divine family. That is the God we preach! It explains why we are as we are – families with fathers, children and other relations. God is a "oneness" of a wondrous loving relationship. The living heartbeat behind creation is His. Family love is God-planned for He is the wellspring of all love. *"God is love ... love is of God,"* Scripture declares in 1 John 4:8, 7. In His creation the Creator works out what He is in Himself. The instinct of selfless motherhood is a reflection of the nature of God, perhaps the nearest we can get to an understanding God's pure love.

> *The Father and the Son love each other and the Holy Spirit is the spirit of love in the divine family.*

Let me show you something beautiful in John 1:1, *"In the beginning was the Word, and the Word was with God."* Now John did not use the ordinary Greek for "with" (*met*), which is only applied to two objects (such as two chairs) near to each other. He used '*pros*," which suggests movement towards, coming face to face, a dynamic, active relationship. Jesus did not speak of being one with the Father in a mechanical sense but in the sense of interacting, of two people loving and living as one.

The Creator is the Father and by nature wants children. The Spirit of sonship is always at work throughout the universe *"bringing many sons to glory"* (Hebrews 2:10). That is God's objective and nothing will stop him. He has greater designs than our present families – to unite all families in the universal and eternal Family of God, *"the household of faith"* (Galatians 6:10), which is made up of His twice-born. Paul said, *"I bow my knees to the Father of our Lord Jesus Christ from whom the whole family in heaven and earth is named"* (Ephesians 3:14).

That explains why God will plant one of His born-again children in a family as the "good soil" from which the others can be reached. That important purpose is expressed in Christ's parable of the sower. Jesus explains the meaning of the story with an unexpected comment. The sower sows the Word of God. Then Jesus said, *"But the [seeds] that fell on the good ground are those who, having heard the word with a noble and good heart, keep it and bear fruit with patience"* (Luke 8:15). The seed becomes people and people are the seed, those in whose hearts the seed of God's Word is sown. They carry the divine seed of life wherever they are. It germinates in the family soil and a soul harvest can follow.

Another parable that is often overlooked, is the one about the growing seed.

> *The kingdom of God is as if a man should scatter seed on the ground, and should sleep by night and rise by day, and the seed should sprout, and he himself does not know how. For the earth yields crops by itself: first the blade, then the head, after that the full grain in the head.* (Mark 4:26-28)

The Greek word here for "by itself" is *'automate'*. The Word of God is placed in our heart; we are sown in the family, and "automatically" fruit is produced, although we do not know how.

We are seed. We do not need to try to be seed; it is automatic. We do not have to browbeat the family, pushing religion down each other's throats with every meal, never giving our parents or siblings a moment of respite. *"Let the word of Christ dwell in you richly"* (Colossians 3:16). This will naturally produce fruit. We are to be just what we are, *'Jesus-people'*, being what the word makes us. We do not know how we make an impact but we do. Quite naturally, *"the earth yields crops by itself"* (Mark 4:28). Everybody loves a lover, or so the saying goes. Love Jesus and others sense it. That is how what it should be like in the home. Christ is life and produces life. A gray and gloomy face is no recommendation of salvation.

> *We are seed. We do not need to try to be seed; it is automatic.*

## GOD'S PURPOSE FOR FAMILIES

The devil hates what God plans. That is why so many influences are eroding natural family life today. One of the ominous last-day signs is that children will be *"disobedient to their parents."* It has become almost a national custom for teenagers to rebel, to turn their backs on their home and the parental guidance they need, and to live independently and do as they like, to be *"unloving"* (2 Timothy 3:3). *"Love"* is family life as God set it up at Creation. Satan immediately attacked it as fatal to his fiendish plans and engineered the murder of Abel by his brother.

Nevertheless, everything in Scripture shouts the glorious truth that God has His eye on every family on earth and seeks to bless them. Most of the Old Testament is about one family – the family of Abraham. God began in Abraham's home four thousand years ago, promising "*I will bless you, and all peoples on earth will be blessed through you*" (Genesis 12:2-3). To many people, God is the Great Judge. But why not the Great Blesser? The first thing He ever said about himself to Abraham was that He would bless all families on earth. He certainly does that. He knocks on every door, smiles, and blesses every household into which He is admitted. Saying "Bless you!" is not just a superstitious response when someone sneezes, but an echo of that living promise of God, "*I will bless you.*" To know what that "blessing" is, we have only to read the story of Abraham – and what an astounding story it is!

> *Scripture shouts the glorious truth that God has his eye on every family.*

I do not think that the members of Abraham's family ever proved particularly worthy. The three patriarchs (Abraham, Isaac, and Jacob) were not model saints, especially Jacob. It is therefore quite surprising that God made them such an example of His blessing. Why did He favor them? First, He was determined to do so, and second, because that family had faith in God. It was the only one on earth at that time that did and they really wanted that blessing. Jacob was a cheat and stole the blessing that should have rightfully gone to the elder son, Esau. Jacob paid dearly for his deceitful behavior. Nevertheless, what strikes us in that incredible story is that he (Jacob) believed that he had received the promised blessing despite the way he went about it.

We are given a clearer example of the desire for God's blessing in 1 Chronicles 4:10: "*Jabez called on the God of Israel saying, "Oh, that You would bless me and enlarge my territory ... So God granted him what he requested.*" By the same token God will bless us – you, me, and our families!

191

We are the special focus of God's concern and attention and so, as Jesus said, there is no need to worry. He will take care of us – not least because of His own spontaneous promise to bless us. Why doubt it? Scripture says that when God could not swear by anybody greater, He swore by Himself (Hebrews 6:13), making a covenant of blessing. He has kept His covenant down the ages, and is not about to change.

## THE NEW FAMILY

The Lord introduced the greatest possible world-change in family life. Christ did not teach much about families, but He had plenty to say about the new Family. His primary concern was with the new order. For example, when Jesus was told that His mother and brothers were outside, wanting to speak to Him, He answered, *"Who is My mother, and who are My brothers?" And He stretched out His hand toward His disciples, and said, "Here are My mother and My brothers! For whosoever does the will of My Father in heaven is My brother and sister and mother"* (Matthew 12:48-50).

Jesus taught us about an intimate relationship with the Father who seeks children of his own kind for his special family. Jesus' habit of calling God "Father" was a new revelation; none of Israel's prophets had spoken of God in such terms. To them the Lord was the Creator-Savior, but Jesus exposed the very nature of God and opened up the greatest of changes and possibilities.

*We are the special focus of God's concern and attention. He will take care of us*

He said, *"You must be born again."* It startled and bewildered the rabbi Nicodemus, who was the first person to whom Jesus revealed this truth (John 3:1-10). From the day of Pentecost and the coming of the Holy Spirit, people were *"born of the Spirit."* Peter saw it,

and saw people experiencing it. He wrote, *"Having been born ag*
*not of corruptible seed, but incorruptible"* (1 Peter 1:23), and later ad
that, through Christ's promises, we *"may be partakers of the di*
*nature, having escaped the corruption that is in the world through*
(2 Peter 1:4).

## OPTING OUT OR OPTING IN

This is all a marvel, but what is even more thrilling is that
happening now, the world over. It is something so special th
needs more than omnipotence. The possibility of being united
God came about only by the sacrifice, blood and work of our
Christ Jesus, and applied by the Holy Spirit. God is bonding bel
in a new way, making brothers and sisters in the family of
one in Christ. We talk of relatives being "consanguine", me
"of one blood", and we say that "blood is thicker than v
However, true human "oneness" is generated by the blood of
God has not finished creation until He makes us *"new cre*
(2 Corinthians 5:17).

We do not choose our nationality or our parents, but God
nobody in his new creation family unless they want to be in
only possible to become a member of his family by secon
We either believe or we do not. We choose to belong eithe
old temporal order or to the new eternal order. That is
greatest issue. God has no elite. His purposes are not
but inclusive. He did not find us as strangers for, *"He*
*His own"* (John 1:11). He bothers with us all, very much
paid the price of bothering, emptying Himself, His hear
at the Cross. After that, if we do not bother, nothing car
for us. There is no other doorbell to ring except that of "*C*
*in heaven*" (Matthew 6:9). We can opt out or opt in.

To come into the eternal Family, to receive Jesus Christ, is how God intended things to be. In fact, it is something perfectly natural – or supernatural. It does not need an emotional trauma, hysteria, or even a special atmosphere. On Paul's missionary journeys, people received Christ into their lives as the result of a straightforward decision. For example, we read that in Athens *"some men joined him and believed"* (Acts 17:34), and in Berea (a place in northern Greece called Verria today) that *"they received the word with all readiness, and searched he Scriptures daily to find out whether these things were so"* (Acts 17:11). As a result, many people believed. God made us for Himself. Christians are the God-planned norm. The godless and Christless have distorted the divine intentions; they are abnormal, freaks, not "in the image of God."

> *To come into the eternal Family, to receive Jesus Christ, is how God intended things to be.*

## PERFECT DESTINY

There is a lovely warmth about the Father's work. Jesus talked about heaven as a home, *"In my Father's house are many mansions"* (John 14:2), places where people can live, family centers. God's sons and daughters have a home ready for them at the end of their journey. The future is not populated by bloodless spirits, unrelated, cold, clinging to the outer edge of existence. The Bible, the picture is of a warm, gathered household where everyone feels at home so that, *"In the ages to come He might show the exceeding riches of His grace in His kindness toward us in Christ Jesus"* (Ephesians 2:7).

The sons of God have the perfect destiny; they have been designed for a God-made future. There is no other future, anyway. We either steer in that direction or have no direction other than that of following a mirage, false trails, paths that circle back on themselves. Those are the

godless ways offered by money, self-gratification, power, prominence and pride, hard paths that peter out in a trackless eternity.

God is the architect of His own purposes. Nothing we can do can disrupt His plans. He makes His family inheritors of glory, light, life, and wonder. Jesus said that we will sit at His table and be waited on (Luke 12:37). This is the Christian hope. It is not an alternative hope – there is no other.

## INHERITANCE RIGHTS

Coming into the family of God is an occasion to celebrate. Perhaps the greatest story told by Jesus, the parable of the lost son, illustrates what a glorious occasion it is to enter the divine family. Of two sons, one leaves home and follows his own devices, only to come back some years later destitute and in rags. As he neared his old home, his elderly father ran to meet him, risking a heart attack, and smothered the young man's apologies with kisses. Jesus said that an occasion like that releases festivity even in heaven: *"I say to you, there is joy in the presence of the angels of God over one sinner who repents"* (Luke 15:10).

*The sons of God have the perfect destiny; they have been designed for a God-made future.*

When we become born-again children of God, we are handed inheritance rights. *"God sent forth His Son ... that we might receive the adoption as sons ... and if a son, then an heir of God through Christ"* (Galatians 4:4-7). We receive the Holy Spirit, the fullness of Christ. God confers upon us the honor of bearing the name of Christ, and calls us to be his fellow workers, His agent-friends, and to know His secrets (John 15:14-16). We are given the kingdom of God (Luke 12:32, 22:29; Matthew 5:3). God gives us many guarantees –

His overshadowing presence, daily care, eternal life, a living hope, a glorious and positive future, a place in His home, and permanent access to the throne-room of God at all times. God never patronizes us or merely tolerates us. He *"remembers no more"* our sins and lawless deeds, and embraces us as His dear children, *"justified from all things"* (Acts 13:39).

*Jesus was born, grew up, was subject to parents, worked and lived for thirty years as the family breadwinner.*

The Bible is full of family warmth. For example, Jesus raised a widow's only son from the dead, but He did not claim him as a member of His entourage to show him off as a miracle. He gave the man back to his mother (Luke 7:11-15). That was significant because when Elijah and Elisha each raised a dead son to life, they both did the same, handing the boys back to their mothers (1 Kings 17:17-23; 2 Kings 4:32-37). Again, when Jesus expelled demons from a madman, the overjoyed man did not want to leave Jesus. He asked if he could go with Him, but Jesus said, *"Go home to your friends, and tell them what great things the Lord has done for you, and how He has had compassion on you"* (Mark 5:19).

Perhaps it is worth reminding ourselves that Jesus did not descend from heaven as an adult. He was born, grew up, was subject to parents, worked and lived for thirty years as the family breadwinner. We do not know when Joseph, Mary's husband and the head of the household, died but Jesus had obviously assumed his role as the first-born son. Even when suffering indescribable torture on the cross, he arranged a home for Mary his mother (John 19:27).

## SOLVING THE PHILOSOPHICAL RIDDLE

When Jesus taught the disciples to pray saying *"Our Father in heaven"*, He changed human thought. He solved the greatest philosophical riddle of all, the question of why we exist. We are here because we have a Father. We are not orphans in a fatherless universe. Everything therefore relates to our Creator and only God gives things meaning, whether they are kings or carrots, people or planets. Jesus said that your Father in heaven *"makes His sun to rise on the evil and the good, and sends rain on the just and on the unjust"* (Matthew 5:45). The disposition of God is that of a Father. Out of that disposition, He made us all, by love, for love, to love, each of us for His divine embrace and care.

They say everyone remembers where they were when President Kennedy was shot, or when the Twin Towers of the World Trade Center collapsed, and generally everyone remembers when Jesus welcomed them into His family. Jesus invited the first two disciples, John and Andrew, into His home when they were quite young, and they never forgot that moment. As an old man John wrote, *"It was about the tenth hour"* (John 1:39). They recalled being in that idyllic house as the sun went down and Jesus' face was lit by a tiny oil lamp. Jesus belongs to homes, not just to towering masses of sacred stones.

> *Jesus came like a father traveling a long distance just to see His family.*

Jesus came like a father traveling a long distance just to see His family. Otherwise, He had no reason to be here at all. He came to be with us, to redeem and to save us. He loved us, mystery as that certainly is! He stood to gain nothing, except us, earthlings, and, contemplating history, I think that we were really more trouble than we were worth. Jesus sought neither glory nor gain, only people – even the unlovable – to bring many sons to the Father. He wanted His family around Him for ever.

He is still seeking people today, beckoning us to get alongside Him and to bring along our families and friends.

## THE MOUNT EVEREST OF POSSIBILITIES

There is every reason for our families to know Jesus. For a start, God wants us to know Him: *"I will give them a heart to know Me, that I am the Lord"* (Jeremiah 24:7). Seven times in Exodus, God says, *"They will know that I am the Lord"* while Ezekiel contains some seventy references to 'knowing the Lord.'

Normality is oneness with Christ, Him and us together. Our human minds cannot conceive a higher relationship than with God. It is the ultimate, the Everest of possibility. It would be impossible for us to scale those heights unless we are equipped by God who desired it. God descended to our human level in Christ, who said, *"I will draw all peoples to Myself"* (John 12:32). After such divine passion bringing such an opportunity, if we do not want to belong to Him, it can only be because Satan and sin have muddied our view and confused our thinking – except that no one knows what it is like to know Jesus until they actually do. Multitudes do know Jesus, but find the experience impossible to convey. Words are not enough to convey what everlasting life is really like.

## TAKEN UP WITH JESUS

Knowing God is bound to transform anyone's outlook on life. When Paul met the risen Christ on the road to Damascus, he could only tell us that he had seen *"the glory of God in the face of Jesus Christ"* (2 Corinthians 4:6). However, from that moment on everything he had thought important he despised as childish. His life was filled with the knowledge of his love. He adored his Lord and called himself

Christ's slave. Years went by and Jesus was still everything to him and he longed for more: "that I may know Him" (Philippians 3:10).

The effect of coming into the family of God, of meeting Jesus of Nazareth is unforgettable. A devout Jew, Nathaniel of Cana, prejudiced against anything from Nazareth, walked into the presence of Jesus of Nazareth and was immediately so moved that he declared, *"Rabbi, you are the Son of God! you are the King of Israel"* (John 1:49). Many met Christ before they knew who He really was, and were brought to adoration. They were Jews and Jews were brought up not to think of God in human form, but Jews were the first to recognize who Jesus really was.

> *The effect of coming into the family of God, of meeting Jesus of Nazareth is unforgettable.*

Believers are taken up with Jesus – not with debate, dogmas, rules, religious observances, human endeavors to reach some spiritual objective. Their creed is Jesus. Christianity is Christ. He has always attracted intellectuals for His love, not for intellectual interests. Jesus did not come to solve conundrums, but to burst into our lives like the morning sun.

We should look at the Bible itself. It is the world's happiest book. It is with us, not because it is an ancient document preserved through the centuries by the church, but because it is alive. What is alive does not need to be preserved. The Bible is the most read of all contemporary books. It is a fountain, not a stone. Biologists tell us that the primary evidences of life are adaptation and reproduction. The gospel, the good news of Jesus, qualifies. Wherever the gospel seed is scattered, it adapts to the soil, takes root, germinates, and reproduces. The book of Acts speaks like that: *"The word of God grew and multiplied"* (Acts 12:24). When governments make laws against the Bible or the gospel, it is a tribute to its vigor. They may well fear and hate it for it is a living force against untruth and oppression.

The first believers were a few raw fishermen. In less than a hundred generations that handful, as Scripture says, has become like a harvest covering the mountains, in every nation, "reproducing" like no other faith by the power of the gospel and the sheer attractiveness of Jesus. Gospel success comes by the gospel, not by threats, population growth or social pressures: *"The word of the Lord endures forever"* (1 Peter 1:25). Jesus draws all men to himself. He stands with wide open arms saying, "Come to Me!"

There is enough oxygen locked up in the rocks of Mars to restore the planet's atmosphere. There is spiritual oxygen enough in the gospel. A Christian in the home brings in a breath of the fresh air of heaven. There is power in the atom for all the power needs of earth for ever. The gospel *"is the power of God to salvation for everyone who believes"* (Romans 1:16).

## GOD WANTS FAMILIES TO BE SAVED

If you want your family to know the Lord, you are on a winning ticket. God wants it more than you, so you have everything going for you. As the world hovers between life and death, the Lord asks us to cooperate in securing the destiny of millions.

Paul declared to a frightened man, *"Believe on the Lord Jesus, and you will be saved, you and your household"* (Acts 16:31). The story begins at midnight with Paul and Silas in jail in Philippi. God rocked the prison with an earthquake and the jailor expected the prisoners to run away as fast as their legs would carry them. If he lost them, however, he could expect to be sentenced to some horrible execution as a punishment. He drew his sword to kill himself, but, with typical command and presence of mind, Paul called out to reassure the poor man. The jailor's reply was a classic: *"Sirs, what must I do to be saved?"*

Now that is interesting. Calling the apostles "sirs" gave Paul his chance, playing on words. In their language "sir" is the same as "Lord." So the jailor had called them "lords." Paul used the same word: *"Believe in the Lord Jesus Christ, and you will be saved."* The jailor had called on the apostles as lords, but the apostles could not save him – only the Lord of lords could do that. Salvation is not found in a host of lords but in the Lord of Hosts.

> *Salvation is not found in a host of lords but in the Lord of Hosts.*

Now, what about the jailor's "household" being saved? The jailor's household was not a modern nuclear family with its 2.3 children. In those days, a household would consist of grandparents, adult sons and their wives, daughters, servants and slaves. The jailor's faith for salvation could not save anybody else, any more than his drinking water could quench their thirst. Yes, they all were saved, but each by their own confession of Christ. That night, before dawn, each one was baptized, confessing their faith in Christ, the badge of Christian identity. They were not saved second-hand through the jailor's salvation, as God's grandchildren, but each one was "born of God" directly.

Nevertheless, Paul knew what he was promising. In that heathen world, here was "seed" sown in good soil, the family. Long before, a murderer, Cain, had provoked God by demanding, *"Am I my brother's keeper?"* (Genesis 4:9). Yes, he was, but killed him anyway. We are all our brother's keepers. Psalm 68:6 tells us, *"God sets the solitary in families."* He never intended isolation, separation, individualism, but interdependence and mutual responsibility.

Sin had brought disruption, division, hostility, families pitted against families, nations against nations, wars, hatred, and murder. What kind of God would welcome anyone because they committed murder? Jesus said that *"the thief does not come except to steal, and to kill, and to destroy"* (John 10:10). He also said that we either follow Him or are scattered all over the place. We are not intended to slide through this world like a snail, leaving no mark other than a slimy trail. When we follow Christ, He says to us, *"See, I have inscribed you on the palms of My hands; yours walls are continually before Me"* (Isaiah 49:16).

The presence of a Christian can be either unifying or divisive: *"Blessed are the peacemakers"* (Matthew 5:9) contrasts with *"a man's enemies will be those of his own household"*, (Matthew 10:36). Consequently, a child of God can never be without an edge, or ineffective. Believers are bound to make some kind of impact. Our gospel smells of either life or death (2 Corinthians 2:16). John Wesley is reported to have told his preachers that they should make people either glad or mad.

## YOUR FAMILY SHALL BE SAVED

God made families and wishes to save families. "No man is an island" wrote John Donne centuries ago. Jesus prayed to the Father for His disciples, *"that they may be one as We are"* (John 17:11). He wanted that because that is how things were meant to be. In New Zealand, the sheep range across the hills for miles, but Christ Jesus said there would be *"one flock and one shepherd"* (John 10:16). That is His assurance for our families.

John's vision of the gathered family in glory brought him the sound of worship, billions praising God. God's praise needs a multitude because only a multitude of eyes can take in every aspect of what God's character is. Corporate worship is biblical worship.

Each of us views Him from our own unique perspective, knows Him from our own experience, and understands Him with our own appreciation. It took all the multitudes that John saw in his vision to appreciate the wonders of the Lamb on the throne, what He was and what He did. *"The eyes of all look expectantly to You"* (Psalm 145:15). All wonder, everything worth talking about, derives from Him. Every joy is His gift, every true pleasure His invention. He is the endless source of all interest, pleasure, and delight inspiring eternal conversation. He is the fountain of life in all its fullness. To know Him is to know only one part of Him, and it takes everybody, all the families on earth, to know Him – and even then we do not know Him entirely.

> *He is the endless source of all interest, pleasure, and delight inspiring eternal conversation.*

It is not selfish to pray for our own family to be saved. It is natural, as God intended. We are in families for that very reason. *"If anyone does not provide for his own, and especially for those of his household, he has denied the faith and is worse than an unbeliever"* (1 Timothy 5:8). We can paraphrase that and say that if anyone does not pray for his own family, he is worse than an unbeliever. We are indeed our brother's keeper! If you are the head of the household, take the opportunity to build an altar to God every day and attract His presence, protection and prosperity.

The secular world talks about families being the building blocks of society, but building blocks need to be cemented together, not left lying around. Families structure society only when firmly bound together. Only one "cement" on earth can be guaranteed to work – not patriotism, but the gospel.

Caring for one's own is not exclusive, whatever people say, for nothing is more natural than family and racial bonds. Churches are often composed of generations of families, and so they should be, Christian dynasties, stabilizing and assuring. However, if a teenage boy or girl meets up with a non-Christian and eventually marries, that begins dynasties that will be godless for centuries.

> *Blessed is every one who fears the Lord, who walks in His ways ... your children like olive plants all around your table. Thus shall the man be blessed who fears the Lord.* (Psalm 128:1-4)

The war is on. Satanic agents are whittling away at the pillars of society and of the churches. The answer is the witness of the Christian family itself, God blessed, like the house of Abraham and of Jabez. There is no law and no argument against that. *"As for me and my household, we will serve the Lord"* (Joshua 24:15).

‿

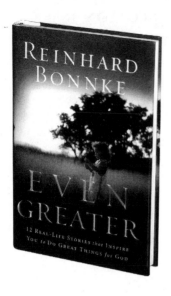

# EVEN GREATER

### 12 REAL-LIFE STORIES that INSPIRE YOU to DO GREAT THINGS for GOD.

OUR DREAMS, LIKE A CHILD'S INNOCENCE ARE IN ESSENCE VERY FRAGILE — BEAUTIFUL TO BEHOLD BUT EASILY BROKEN.

Yet God is larger than a dream, stronger than a fear, and higher than an expectation. *Even Greater* delivers dramatic, faith-building true stories about ordinary people from around the world. People just like you, with whom God did extraordinary works despite broken dreams, failure and weakness. His grace is freely given . . .

YOU WILL BE MOVED . . . YOU WILL BE INSPIRED . . . YOU WILL BE CHALLENGED . . . TO DO EVEN GREATER WORKS FOR GOD!

*God will do amazing things through anyone who is willing to sincerely believe His word. Reinhard Bonnke is a tremendous man of God who through his book, Even Greater, will ignite a passion to accomplish "even greater" things for God than can be imagined.*

- Joyce Meyer, best selling author and Bible teacher

·192 pages
·ISBN 0-9758789-0-5

# The Christian Life Collection is a compilation of previously published booklets:

### The Holy Spirit Baptism

The greatest assurance of all flows from personal experience of the manifestation of God's power. Drawing from Scripture, this carefully explained and simple to understand booklet brings the believer to the place of faith where he or she can receive the baptism of the Holy Spirit. Common misconceptions are answered and the reader is challenged to ask and receive!

·32 pages
·ISBN 3-935057-12-1

### Assurance of Salvation

This booklet tackles the first and most vital crisis that every new believer faces. Before anything else, we must know we are saved! It is the crucial link between salvation and discipleship. Using graphic illustrations from Scripture, this message forms the basis of the booklet *Now that You are Saved*, given to new believers in every CfaN campaign.

·28 pages
·ISBN 3-935057-11-3

### How to Receive a Miracle from God

Perhaps the greatest single obstacle to accepting the reality of miracles is our inability to understand God's dynamics. The dynamics of the miraculous are the Word of God, faith and obedience. When these three are in place, miracles happen. This booklet will unlock the doors of unbelieving hearts to expect a miracle from God.

·24 pages
·ISBN 3-935057-13-X

### First of all ... Intercession

"Evangelism without intercession is like an explosive without a detonator," says Reinhard Bonnke. Christians have a world to reclaim and regain for God. Prayer and intercession cast out the entrenched enemy, violate his borders and retake lost territory. This booklet explains the task of intercession clearly and concisely, and encourages Christians to use the weapon of prayer more consistently and effectively.

·32 pages
·ISBN 3-935057-17-2

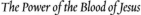

### The Power of the Blood of Jesus

The blood type of Jesus is unique. Since it was spiritually created it has spiritual power. As a young evangelist Reinhard Bonnke vowed that wherever he went he would preach on the blood of Jesus. This booklet contains that powerful gospel message in all its life-changing anointing.

·24 pages
·ISBN 3-935057-10-5

### Faith for the Night

In this booklet Evangelist Reinhard Bonnke explains that faith is like a wiring system that carries power into our lives. Faith itself is not the power, but it links us to the power source. There is no link to God's power without faith!

· 28 pages
· ISBN 3-935057-16-4

### The Lord your Healer

God loves to heal. He still heals today. During CfaN campaigns, we see thousands receive healing and remain totally healed. This straightforward but profound booklet answers the critics and lifts our faith. We do not look to church leaders, special ministries or Reinhard Bonnke for healing, but to Jesus. He will answer.

·24 pages
·ISBN 3-935057-14-8

### The Romance of Redeeming Love

When God gave His Son Jesus to die for us, it cost Him everything. The gift of Redemption is the ultimate expression of God's love. This booklet reveals through Scripture, God's unique and perfect Redemption plan. Creation was easy, but for our Redemption, God gave Himself.

·32 pages
·ISBN 3-935057-15-6

### Winning Your Friends and Family to Christ

Without friends and family you would live a lonely existence. God made you for this interdependence, and the responsibility of caring for one another. In this powerful little booklet, Reinhard Bonnke explores biblical perspectives on personal relationships and the responsibility to share the Gospel to those closest to you. His words will give you the courage to act and steps to become an effective soul winner in your own home and community.

·32 pages
·ISBN 0-9758789-3-X

**CfaN**
CHRIST
**FOR ALL NATIONS**

For further information about the ministry of Reinhard Bonnke or
Christ for all Nations, please visit our website or contact the office
nearest to you;

Christ for all Nations
Postfach 60 05 74
60335 Frankfurt am Main
Germany

Christ for all Nations
Singapore Post Centre Post Office
P.O. Box 418
Singapore 914014

Christ for all Nations
P.O. Box 590588
Orlando
FL 32859-0588, USA

Christ for all Nations
P.O. Box 25057
London, Ontario
N6C 6A8, Canada

Christ for all Nations
250 Coombs Road
Halesowen
West Midlands
B62 8AA, UK

Christ for all Nations
P.O. Box 50015
West Beach, 7449
South Africa

www.CfaN.org

*Full Flame* GmbH

For information about the purchase of other books and booklets by
Reinhard Bonnke contact;

Full Flame, LLC
P.O. Box 593647
Orlando, FL 32859
USA

Full Flame, GmbH
Postfach 60 05 95
60335 Frankfurt am
Main
Germany

Full Flame Asia, Pte Ltd
451 Joo Chiat Road
#03-05
Singapore 472664

info@FullFlameOnline.com
www.FullFlameOnline.com

info@FullFlame.com
www.FullFlame.com

SEA@FullFlame.com
www.FullFlame.com